READY AS YOU ARE

READY AS YOU ARE

Discovering a Life of Abundance
When You Feel Inadequate, Uncertain,
and Disqualified

BRITTANY MAHER &
CASSANDRA SPEER

NELSON
BOOKS

An Imprint of Thomas Nelson

Published in Nashville, Tennessee, by Nelson Books, an imprint of Thomas Nelson. Nelson Books and Thomas Nelson are registered trademarks of HarperCollins Christian Publishing, Inc.

Published in association with The Bindery Agency, www.TheBinderyAgency.com.

Thomas Nelson titles may be purchased in bulk for educational, business, fundraising, or sales promotional use. For information, please email SpecialMarkets@ThomasNelson.com.

ISBN 978-1-4002-3114-0 (HC)
ISBN 978-1-4002-3121-8 (audiobook)
ISBN 978-1-4002-3120-1 (ePub)

Library of Congress Control Number: 2024948870

Printed in the United States of America

24 25 26 27 28 LBC 5 4 3 2 1

*To every woman who has ever felt unseen,
unqualified, or unprepared. This book is for you.
May you find courage to trust that God's timing is
perfect, His plans for you are good, and He has equipped
you for the mission right where you stand today.
May the words in this book embolden you to give
God all that you hold, just as you are, right where
you're at. You are seen, called, and needed.*

CONTENTS

INTRODUCTION

Hey, friend.

Have you ever felt an unexplainable pull toward something greater for your life? Like there has to be something more? A purpose perhaps long forgotten, or buried deep beneath layers of doubt, apprehension, and idleness? You are not alone.

We are two women who have grappled with our own significance for years. Call it imposter syndrome or lack of identity—we've been there, and we understand the struggle is *real*.

We've questioned and doubted.
We've been at war for our worth.
We've struggled with our purpose.
We've lived in periods of stagnation and idleness.
We've believed lies that have held us back from moving
forward into what God has so graciously laid
before us.

We get it.

Even though we all come to these pages from different walks of life, carrying our unique burdens, dreams, doubts, delays, and joys, we're united by our path through a world that often leaves us with more questions than answers—questions about our purpose, our calling, our struggles, and how we see ourselves in God's grand story.

Should I be doing something more amazing for God? If I do feel a nudge toward something, am I ready? Am I truly qualified? Am I even allowed to do this?

These questions have often echoed in the corridors of our minds, like a lingering melody that refuses to fade. They aren't just hypothetical; they're the kind that nudge us awake at night. They might even be the ones holding us back, planting seeds of fear and confusion, entangling our steps or freezing us in our tracks.

For many of us, especially as women, these questions could also be accompanied by other questions:

Am I enough?
Am I too much?
Too uneducated?
Am I too lacking?
Too different?
Too imperfect?
Too broken?
Does my gender define or confine my capabilities?

We grapple with these questions in the quiet corners of our bedrooms, office spaces, churches, and in the noisy chaos of households. They linger as we transition from one role to another—daughter, friend, student, professional, wife, mother, leader—each bringing its own set of expectations, joys, challenges, and heartaches.

If you are like us, you may have struggled to think your life's purpose is some event far in the future because of lack of clarity in the now. Thoughts like:

When I graduate school, then I'll be ready.
When I meet that special someone, then . . .
When I get married, then . . .
When I have kids, then . . .
When I get that job, then . . .
When I hit that milestone, then . . .
When I get an invitation, then . . .

We punt our purpose into the future, as though we couldn't possibly live with purpose today. The reality of our purpose can sometimes feel like a distant dream, out of reach. But what if an invitation has already been extended?

What if, amid the noise, God is whispering to us a purpose for where we stand?

What if purpose is possible in the here and now?

What if we lean into that whisper today?

Through the years, we've learned to embrace our present

moments as a vital part of our journeys toward purposeful living, finding His beauty to behold in our struggles, faithfully wrestling with our doubts and waiting periods. By no means have we arrived, but we are learning to walk in purpose daily. God is steadily unveiling His plan in our everyday moments and in the future we're stepping into.

And the same can be true for you. Let us gently remind you of who you are and your significance right now.

We are the hands and feet of Christ. That's no small matter, friend! To think we get to be the hands and feet of the Savior of the world? What a beautiful responsibility, and one we get to walk in right now.

Remember what the apostle Paul wrote in Ephesians 2:10: "We are his workmanship, created in Christ Jesus for good works, which God prepared beforehand, that we should walk in them." In this light, we are each fashioned with purpose, intricately designed to act on the good works laid out for us. Whether in seasons of waiting or in the throes of daily chaos, each moment is an opportunity for purposeful action and godly partnership. As we move forward, let's carry this truth with us: Our lives are active tapestries of God's handiwork, and every thread we weave—no matter how insignificant it may seem—contributes to the masterpiece He is creating.

WHETHER IN SEASONS OF WAITING OR IN THE THROES OF DAILY CHAOS, EACH MOMENT IS AN OPPORTUNITY FOR PURPOSEFUL ACTION AND GODLY PARTNERSHIP.

To the woman who feels like she's living in a constant season of waiting, there's a purpose for where your feet are today. Your life isn't on hold; God has an intentional plan for you. Purpose can be found in the here and now.

To the mom whose hair is a tangled mess while running around her house with spit-up on her clothing, tending to her children's needs, there's purpose where your feet are. You're raising little disciples, and that is a huge deal to God. What you do matters beyond what you can see.

To the girl whose grief threatens to steal her joy, there are no words we could say that could soothe the loss you've endured, but allow us to encourage you with this truth: God sees you, He cares about you, and He is working in every situation.

To the woman who puts in a whopping fifty-plus-hour workweek, surviving off microwaved meals and wondering if this really is it for your life, there is so much purpose where your feet are. Your mission right now is where you're placed. Your hard work and dedication do not go unnoticed. Keep doing it all unto Him.

To the woman who wonders if her best days are behind her, don't miss the beauty of the present by yearning for yesterday. There's purpose found in living with expectancy today.

And to the girl tirelessly searching for her calling while still in school, there are great things ahead of you, yes, but don't forsake where you're at now with Jesus. One is not greater than the other. This moment is important too.

In this book, we want to come alongside you and wrestle

through your questions—to explore the depths of our purpose in both the grand and the everyday. We want to help you stop waiting to participate in what God is doing right now. We want to help you embrace the here and find joy in the now, while still anticipating the future as we await the Lord's return.

If you've ever felt lost, confused, uncertain, or in need of direction, we encourage you to keep reading. This book is more than just words on a page written in black and white: It's a promise of discovery, of uncovering His purpose woven into every aspect of your life right now.

Are you ready?

ONE

PURPOSE DOESN'T HAVE TO BE CONFUSING

Exploring the concept of purpose is much like embarking on a voyage across the vast seas. Before setting sail, it's essential to understand what anchors your ship and guides your journey. Purpose acts as both the anchor and the compass—it's the driving force behind our actions, the reason we rise in the morning, and the quiet resolve that sustains us through trials.

Before we delve into the depths of purpose and the day-to-day living of it, let's lay the foundation by exploring what *purpose* truly means. Purpose, in its essence, is the unique blueprint God crafts for each of our lives—a combination of divine design and personal calling. This journey of purpose

THIS JOURNEY OF PURPOSE ISN'T A PATH WALKED IN ISOLATION; IT'S A SHARED PILGRIMAGE WHERE OUR INDIVIDUAL STORIES WEAVE INTO THE LARGER TAPESTRY OF GOD'S PLAN.

isn't a path walked in isolation; it's a shared pilgrimage where our individual stories weave into the larger tapestry of God's plan. But how do we discover this purpose, and more importantly, how do we know when we've found it? These are the questions we must address as we embark on this exploration. Let's start by taking a look at the bigger picture.

MACRO PURPOSE AND MICRO PURPOSE

Imagine standing on a sandy shore, gazing out at a vast horizon, and then blasting up five thousand feet. From your vantage point, you can see the entire beautiful landscape where the sky meets the sea. This expanse before you paints a picture of God's macro purpose for your life.

What we're calling macro purpose is God's large-scale, overarching purpose for you. It's the legacy you're called to leave, the mark you imprint on the earth, and the echoes of your existence that will resonate beyond your time. It's reminiscent of Jeremiah 29:11, where the Lord declares, "I know the plans I have for you . . . plans to prosper you and not to harm you, plans to give you hope and a future" (NIV). It encompasses the grand mission He has in mind, including the summation of your actions and choices. It's rooted in God's will for you, characterized by moments of growth, challenge, and triumph, while fulfilling a greater purpose within His grand design. This is a journey He has penned for you and for us. We need only to abide and give our yes. Because, truly, our decisions matter. We can either participate in what God is doing or we can choose not to. It's up to us to decide.

As we consider the concept of macro purpose, let's not overlook the beauty and significance of the micro purpose in our lives. Back to the sandy-shore analogy for a moment. Once you come back down from the sky, your feet back on the shore, your focus narrows as you gaze at the horizon before you. You see the path beneath your feet, feel the sand between your toes, notice the flowers by the wayside—all the small details that together make up the bigger view you'd been taking in before. This is micro purpose. We live it out in the simple acts, the everyday routines, and the small moments of joy and challenge through which we live out our purpose.

Micro purpose is where the grand narrative of our macro purpose becomes tangible and actionable. It's where we experience the depth of our calling through the relationships we build, the people we serve, and the love we share. In the quiet whispers of the spirit, in the gentle nudges toward action, and in the daily decisions we face, we find the micro moments that define our faith and our walk with God.

It's the daily grind for the season you are currently in. It's purpose for today. The here and the now. Purpose for where you are currently planted. It's being present in the present, acknowledging the sacred in the secular, and finding God in the ordinary. It's our day-to-day walk, where every decision, every act of obedience, and every intentional and unintentional moment matters.

As we progress on our journey, let's embrace each day as an opportunity to live out our macro and micro purposes. Let's find joy in the journey, peace in the process, and purpose in every step.

Too often we see the highlight reels of others—we see them accomplishing their macro purposes—and we get stuck thinking that purpose has to be grand. But in reality, the grandest purposes are often lived out through the smallest acts of kindness, the quietest moments of sacrifice, and the humblest acts of service. It's the unseen hours of prayer, the unnoticed acts of kindness, and the uncelebrated moments of perseverance that forge the character required for such accomplishments. It's the behind-the-scenes, the early mornings, the late nights, and the perseverance in the unseen that carves the path to our greater calling.

Need some examples to help you understand the way macro and micro purposes work together? Let's take a look at a few people from the Bible.

The Life of Esther

Take the example of Esther. Esther's macro purpose was her crucial role in saving the Jewish people from genocide. She was an orphaned Jewish girl who became the queen of Persia, and God placed her in a position of influence "for such a time as this" (Esther 4:14). Her queenship and her bold intervention with the king to prevent the execution of her people reflect the large, overarching purpose God had for her life. It was a purpose that had significant implications for the history of the Jewish people.

Esther's micro purpose can be seen in her everyday actions leading up to her pivotal moment. For instance, her daily choices in the king's palace, her approach to winning the favor of those around her, and the steps she took to reveal Haman's plot without putting herself or her people in immediate danger. These included fasting, prayer, and carefully planning the banquets where she would plead for her people's lives. Each of these small, intentional acts was critical in fulfilling her macro purpose of delivering her people from destruction.

By understanding both macro and micro purposes, believers can develop a more nuanced understanding of their roles in the kingdom of God. It won't be one-size-fits-all. It will be more of a personalized approach to fulfilling the Great Commission and glorifying God in all we do—in the everyday.

As Luke 16:10 reminds us, "One who is faithful in a very little is also faithful in much." Our macro and micro purposes intertwine and go hand in hand. They both matter. Being faithful in the daily, seemingly small matters aligns us more closely

BEING FAITHFUL IN THE DAILY, SEEMINGLY SMALL MATTERS ALIGNS US MORE CLOSELY WITH GOD'S GREAT MACRO PURPOSE FOR OUR LIVES.

with God's great macro purpose for our lives. We can't focus so much on the macro that we miss the opportunities right in front of us. Friend, each day presents countless opportunities to live faithfully and to act with intention.

The Life of Joseph

Consider the life of Joseph, son of Jacob. We can see distinct examples of both macro and micro purposes when we look at his path.

Joseph's macro purpose unfolded as he rose from slavery to become the second-most-powerful man in Egypt. His overarching mission was to preserve a remnant of people during a severe famine, as stated in Genesis 45:7: "God sent me before you to preserve for you a remnant on earth, and to keep alive for you many survivors." This plan was not just for Egypt's benefit but was crucial for the survival of the future nation of Israel, his own family.

Joseph's micro purpose is evident in his everyday faithfulness and integrity, regardless of his circumstances. When he was sold into slavery, he served Potiphar diligently, resulting in being put in charge of Potiphar's entire household. In prison, Joseph interpreted dreams for Pharaoh's cupbearer and baker (Genesis 40), a small act that would later lead to his rise to power. These everyday actions and decisions, rooted in his faith in God, were instrumental in achieving the larger purpose God had for him.

Joseph's story demonstrates how the micro purposes—his consistent character, his responses to injustice and hardship, and his management of small responsibilities—were all foundational in achieving the macro purpose God set for his life, which had lasting implications for the entire Hebrew people and the fulfillment of God's promises.

Each of our lives, in essence, dances to the rhythm of these two dimensions of purpose. And to truly embrace what God has laid out for each one of us, we must learn to appreciate His grand narrative for us while also valuing each moment with Him that crafts our unique story. Because the truth is, our days here are numbered. This isn't our home, and spoiler alert: Jesus is coming back. So, what we do here with our time—it really matters.

SHARED VERSUS INDIVIDUAL PURPOSE

Another part of this framework for purpose is shared versus individual purpose. These are each a particular type of micro purpose, a more specific category of the day-to-day activities we engage in.

So what's the difference then between shared micro purpose and individual micro purpose?

Within God's purpose for the world is a shared purpose that all believers obtain when we say yes to Jesus. When we're talking about shared purpose, we're referring to the collective aims and responsibilities that are universally applicable to all believers within the body of Christ. These are the fundamental principles every believer is called to embody and practice, such as spreading the gospel, making disciples, loving one another, serving others, and glorifying God. Shared purpose represents the common mission and objectives that unite believers in our faith and actions.

Our shared purpose includes:

Getting Saved. He wants all people to be saved and to come to the knowledge of the truth (1 Timothy 2:4).

Glorifying God. This is the ultimate aim of our lives—to glorify God in all we do (1 Corinthians 10:31).

Spreading the Gospel. Sharing the good news of Jesus Christ is a commission given to all believers (Mark 16:15).

Making Disciples. Discipleship is about more than conversion; it's about helping others grow in their faith too (Matthew 28:19–20).

Loving One Another. Jesus stressed the importance of loving one another as a central tenet of Christian life (John 13:34–35).

Serving Others. Following the example of Jesus, we are to serve others selflessly (Matthew 20:26–28).

Shining Brightly. All believers were made to shine brightly for the world to see, giving glory to the Father (Matthew 5:16).

Imitating God. He wants all believers to imitate Him in love (Ephesians 5:1).

Representing God to the World. We are called to be ambassadors of Christ, representing Him to the world around us (2 Corinthians 5:20).

Choosing Life. This encompasses the idea of making
choices that not only honor God but also contribute
to a full, meaningful life (Deuteronomy 30:19–20).

We could add much more to this list, but you get the point.
These callings represent a shared, high-level purpose for all
believers. If you don't yet know what your purpose is, at least
you'll have these shared-purpose items to guide you until the
picture becomes clearer.

Individual purpose, on the other hand, involves the unique,
specific calling or mission that God has for each believer, distinct from the shared purposes of the Christian community. It
represents how a person applies the broader, shared purpose
in their own life, influenced by their personal gifts, skills, circumstances, and life stage. Individual purpose can encompass
a wide range of activities, roles, and ministries tailored to each
person's divine calling and how they contribute to God's kingdom in a way only they can.

Individual purposes could include any of the following:

Specific Career Path. Whether you're a server,
musician, customer service rep, doctor, artist, or
entrepreneur, your vocation can be a means to fulfill
your individual purpose.

Parenting. For some, the call to raise godly children is
their primary individual purpose.

Community. Some are specifically called to impact

their local community through social programs, evangelism, and so on.

Unique Ministries. Whether it's through a music, writing, or speaking ministry, God may have a specific avenue for you to impact others for Christ.

Mentorship. Your purpose may include providing spiritual and life guidance to specific individuals.

Financial Stewardship. God has blessed some individuals with the financial means to support various ministries and charitable works.

Serving. Serving can take many forms, such as someone serving in the church or at home in their family, and more. We are all called to serve in the body of Christ. How has God called you to serve?

This list could be infinite, but again, you get the point.

While our shared purposes serve as the collective heartbeat of the Christian community, our individual purposes are the unique expressions of life and service that God orchestrates in each of our stories. They are the personalized ways we live out the broader callings—infused with our character, experiences, and passions. It's essential to recognize that your individual purpose doesn't exist in isolation but is a harmonious part of the grand symphony of God's kingdom, where every note contributes to the divine melody.

Like we've stated earlier in this chapter, the problem that keeps us from making the most of both our shared purpose and our individual purposes is that too often we can become captivated by and fixated on the larger, overarching narrative of our life—the macro purpose. This vision, as grand as it is, can overshadow the minute yet crucial decisions we make every day—our micro purpose. These daily choices, though seemingly small in the moment, are like beautiful individual brushstrokes to a final masterpiece. His final masterpiece. By overlooking them, we risk missing out on the beauty of the walk and the lessons God has placed along the way to help us grow.

We know it's really easy to become enamored by the end goal, but as we navigate the path to our God-given macro purpose, we should hold these words close to our hearts: "The heart of man plans his way, but the LORD establishes his steps" (Proverbs 16:9). This verse captures the dynamic between our macro purpose and all the micro steps God has called us to take. We might have a grand plan in our hearts—and that's okay—but it is through daily obedience and submission to God's will that we truly walk in alignment with His purpose.

Another testament to the power of our daily decisions comes from Jesus Himself. He taught, "Seek first the kingdom of God and his righteousness, and all these things will be added to you. Therefore do not be anxious about tomorrow, for tomorrow will be anxious for itself. Sufficient for the day is its own trouble" (Matthew 6:33–34). This verse is a powerful reminder to me (Britt) to focus on the present moment. This very moment is the only moment that is real. So, what will I do with it? I want to prioritize making the most of my micro purpose right now while simultaneously trusting God with the macro.

Rest in this: the ordinary, seemingly insignificant acts of obedience we walk in daily will act as the seeds we sow, nurturing our journey toward a bountiful harvest that awaits us in the future. In the dance between the daily and the divine, every act of kindness, each moment of courage, and all choices of faithfulness are the brushstrokes that paint the grand picture of our lives. The macro and the micro aspects of our purpose are not separate journeys we're on but one continuous path where each step is guided by God's hand.

As we walk out our days, let's hold fast to the truth that in God's eyes there are no small roles or insignificant days. Every choice for kindness, every act of service, and every moment of faithfulness is significant in building the life He envisions for us. Keep faith in the small steps, for they lead to the fulfillment of great plans He has promised. Lean into the present, cherishing each encounter and task as an integral part of your purpose, and watch as the seeds of today blossom into the harvest of tomorrow.

REFLECTION QUESTIONS

1. How can recognizing both your macro and micro purposes help you make sense of your daily experiences and choices as part of God's larger plan for your life?
2. How does the story of Esther inspire you to find purpose in both the ordinary and extraordinary aspects of your life?
3. Reflect on a time when a small act of kindness or obedience played a significant role in your life. How did this shape your understanding of purpose?
4. How does the concept of shared versus individual purpose help you understand your unique role within the Christian community?

TWO

MORE THAN THE
SPOTLIGHT

It was more than thirteen years ago when I (Britt) was standing on the precipice of a new life with Jesus. As I flipped through the delicate, gold-edged pages of my Bible for the first time, I felt a mix of intimidation and wonder. Especially with the Old Testament. Terms like "burnt offerings" and names I couldn't even pronounce out loud had me scratching my head! The stories it held—of Moses making waves (literally) and Esther's courageously bold heart to stand up for her people—felt like they were pulled from an epic movie script or some sort of superhero tale. And it got me thinking: *Shouldn't I be doing big things like that too?* To me, with my lack of understanding at the time, these grand stories felt like benchmarks I needed to be trying to duplicate in some way. Maybe they have felt that way for you too?

I think such narratives can often lead us as Christians to believe that to truly matter in God's grand plan our lives must mirror these beautifully colossal tales. We may start to feel that—in order to be of any significance or to fulfill God's ultimate design for us—our stories must parallel the grand ones in the Bible or the grand stories of the lives of other Christians around us. I've personally fallen prey to this.

Our culture has a prevalent narrative that we must be constantly in pursuit of something big, something that gets noticed, to make an impact or to live a life of significance. It's as if our worth and purpose are measured by the scale of our achievements or the visibility of our successes.

We find ourselves worn out and running on empty, forgetting the importance of now. Ecclesiastes 1:14 poignantly describes this as "chasing after the wind," a pursuit that is ultimately futile and unsatisfying (NIV). He must have more for us.

The truth we need to embrace is that there is so much more for us than this relentless grind. Our significance isn't dependent on whether we're living out some grand, ultimate design that we or society have crafted. In fact, by focusing solely on the grand, we risk missing the powerful work God is doing in the small.

We want to make something clear here: We all have the same deep longing to belong and to matter to the world around us. Each of us lives with that repetitive itching question that pulsates within our souls: *Lord, what is my purpose, and why am I here?* We believe our Creator made us this way. To seek after

Him fiercely, and to desire to live out our faith in a loud way that makes an impact on the world around us—this is embedded in our spiritual DNA. To wonder beyond the now, to dream. This yearning isn't random. And yet, the ordinary and the everyday obedience is where much of our true purpose is realized.

The importance of this unsung day-to-day obedience often goes unnoticed and is dangerously overlooked. It's filled with an understated strength and opportunity for quiet obedience. Too often, our distractions from the wrong things can lead us to miss it. Though we know God uses each of us in unique and mighty ways, there's so much beauty to behold in allowing Him to shape us in the here and now.

What do we mean by the "here and now"? It's what nobody else sees. Those moments that are just between you and Jesus. We believe that through seeking Him in those moments, we unveil the truth that it's less about "what am I here to do?" and more about "who am I here to be—right now, moment by moment?"

God's plan for us isn't always about the limelight. Actually, His best work is often done in the background. *Phew*, what a relief. We can have deep significance in the body of Christ, even without the appearance of living in what the world sees as grand. In fact, more often than not, it's about the quiet and the consistency of cultivating a heart fully attuned to

GOD'S PLAN FOR US ISN'T ALWAYS ABOUT THE LIMELIGHT. ACTUALLY, HIS BEST WORK IS OFTEN DONE IN THE BACKGROUND.

Him. The results that come from that, whether small or grand, will help our cups overflow (Psalm 23:5).

THE GENTLE AND LOWLY PATH

Significance in God's kingdom is often found in quiet moments, away from the gaze of the world. In this space, we learn the profound value of small, faithful steps taken in obedience and humility, steps that may never be lauded by others but are nonetheless glorious in the eyes of the One we serve. Really, all God wants is a heart that is attuned to Him and after His own heart.

You don't need a ministry title or a large audience on social media to be an asset to the kingdom. Nor do you need public validation to confirm God's work within you. After all, who are these displays of faithfulness for in the first place? Isn't our obedience and relationship with Him the true reward? It should be.

We must be careful not to make a performance out of our obedience to God. Matthew 6:1 warns, "Be careful not to practice your righteousness in front of others to be seen by them. If you do, you will have no reward from your Father in heaven" (NIV). While it might seem like it does, this doesn't contradict Jesus' previous command to let your light shine before men (Matthew 5:16). Yes, Christians are likely to be seen doing good works out in the world simply because we are called to serve others, but the issue here is the motivation. When it becomes about doing good simply to be seen by the world, it is no longer following a calling but pursuing a selfish ambition.

This isn't to imply that our diligence and good works should be hidden, but we want to make an important distinction as to why we do what we do. Motives matter. If affirmation, attention, and applause are the source of our true motivation, we willingly forfeit a reward in heaven. The fleeting approval and admiration of others becomes our only reward. God cares about how we serve Him and what motivates our actions.

The idea that important work needs to be widely affirmed has ensnared many in the body of Christ today. The pull toward achievements, recognition, and prominence can be strong. And, hey, it's not horrible to desire those things, but we must always remember the source of our true calling and worth. It's not the accolades or the titles but our relationship with Jesus and what He did on the cross for us.

Let's pause for a moment and reflect on this verse: "Take my yoke upon you, and learn from me, for I am gentle and lowly in heart, and you will find rest for your souls. For my yoke is easy, and my burden is light" (Matthew 11:29–30). We find it incredibly breathtaking that when Jesus chose to describe His very nature, He didn't speak of grandeur or might. Instead, He depicted Himself as "gentle and lowly."

This reminds us that in God's kingdom, the last will eventually be first and those who lead will humbly serve. Let's not forget this. What is our motive? Is it the grand path or the gentle and lowly path? What would it look like for us to dial back a little bit and not be so desperate to be used in what we perceive to be a "mighty way"? What about the humble act of washing feet, prioritizing your sister's needs over yours, or stepping aside to let someone else go first? These teachings starkly contrast with the values our society often upholds—a society that places "me" at the center of everything.

What is Jesus' call for us? It's a call to lay down our self-centered desires and live a life filled with and reflecting His selfless love.

Remember, friend, our walks are about way more than the big, noticeable moments that capture attention; they're equally rooted in the collection of small acts of obedience, the daily surrender, and the heart that says yes to God even when the path ahead is unclear. It's the gentle and lowly road, the narrow path, the one that feels small, that leads to the greater road ahead.

If the world doesn't see you doing anything significant by their standards, it does not mean you are insignificant. What if you are exactly where He wants you?

Every "grand" individual in the Bible also had countless days of quiet trust, patience, and commitment to God's will. Days that I'm sure were filled with long windows of waiting, with small decisions that might have seemed trivial but were pivotal in His plan.

As we walk closely with Jesus each day, we can feel content knowing He's guiding us and that's truly enough. And in the place of faithful, small steps that are not so grand, everything falls into place.

FROM PASTURES TO PALACES

Picture this: beautiful rolling hills covered by flocks of sheep grazing and a young man with sun-kissed skin, dirt beneath his fingernails, and the musky scent of sheep lingering on him. This was David's world, a world away from politics, wars, and crowns. A simple, rustic life. Yet within this setting, the heart of a king was being molded.

You see, being a shepherd wasn't a glamorous job. It was humble work that demanded patience, bravery, and a sense of responsibility. David was the youngest son in his family, possibly overlooked by his brothers, and given the least desirable job. But it was here, amid the sheep, that David developed a relationship with God that was pure, authentic, and intimate.

Remember the stories of him defending his flock from a lion and a bear (1 Samuel 17:34–37)? It wasn't just about his physical strength (though, no doubt that was impressive!); it was a testament to his character. A shepherd's duty was to protect, and David took that responsibility to heart.

Then there was that pivotal day when the prophet Samuel visited his home (1 Samuel 16). Initially, David wasn't even considered when Samuel asked David's father to bring his sons to him. David was out, doing his duty, tending to the sheep. Yet, when he was finally called in and stood before Samuel, God made it clear: this was the chosen one. Not because of his stature or impressive resume but because of his heart.

It's wonderful how God described David as "a man after his

own heart" (1 Samuel 13:14). Just think about that for a second. Out of all the accolades and titles David would later earn—giant slayer, warrior, king—this intimate acclamation from God stands out and surpasses them all. It's echoed throughout the ages.

Why David? What set him apart? It was his heart that was shaped in the solitude and humble beginnings of the pastures. A heart that sought God in simplicity and truth, a heart that sang praises in the stillness of the night, a heart that trusted God even when faced with giants.

David's journey from shepherd to king is a testament to God's way of seeing things. While people look at outward appearances, God looks at the heart. David wasn't perfect; he had his share of flaws and made tremendous mistakes (as do we all), but his heart was always tuned to God, always repentant and seeking after Him.

So, when you feel like you're in your shepherd phase of humble beginnings, remember David. It's not necessarily about where you are now but where your heart is. Is it after God's heart? God, the Creator of heaven and earth, can certainly take you from the pastures to the palace, from the background to the forefront, but it all starts with having a heart that genuinely seeks Him, not the palaces.

At the end of the day, while palaces and crowns can be captivating to the flesh, they're not the ultimate prize. It's easy to become infatuated with the idea of reaching our "palaces"—those big moments or achievements we dream of. But if we become too fixated on them, we might miss out on the beauty and lessons in the simplicity of the present.

My friend, wherever you are, right here and right now, there's something to behold, something to learn, and a heart to be shaped. Remember, it's not just about where we are going but who we are becoming along the way. Just like David, let's ensure our hearts are always tuned to Him, whether we're in the pastures, on the battlegrounds, or in the palace.

IT'S NOT JUST ABOUT WHERE WE ARE GOING BUT WHO WE ARE BECOMING ALONG THE WAY.

FAITHFULNESS OVER FAME

Have you read the parable of the lost sheep in Matthew 18:12–14? It talks about how the shepherd leaves his ninety-nine sheep to find the one that is lost, and likewise, God does the same with us. Every time I (Britt) read these words, a sense of comfort washes over me. It's not just the idea that He searches tirelessly for His lost sheep, but that He deeply values each and every individual soul. Even just the one.

This truth has been a guide in our ministry, Her True Worth. When I started it back in 2015, I had this feeling in my heart that we would have a team with many leaders. I never sought to make this an avenue for fame but rather an opportunity to walk in obedience and faithfulness to minister to "the one" person.

That became a driving force for me—the one. And that's what ended up drawing me to Cass when I stumbled upon her on Instagram.

We hadn't met in person. She was a total stranger. As I was praying for a team at this time, something drew me to her ministry. She had a modest following, and the way she faithfully nurtured what God had given her stood out to me. Her words were more than just letters on a digital screen; they were God-breathed and always aimed at reaching "the one." In a world obsessed with followers, likes, numbers, and strategy, there's something incredibly refreshing about setting out to minister to just one person.

As Britt mentioned above, I (Cass) have always approached writing with an intended audience of one. I don't think I could've pressed the post button for the first time if I genuinely thought millions of people would be reading my words back then. It's still a bit unnerving even now as I'm typing these words. To tell the truth, I found a level of comfort in thinking hardly anyone would see what I was writing. I felt like I was safely wrapped in a blanket of obscurity.

During the first few years of my writing journey, I was able to build confidence as I wrote, because there weren't a lot of eyes on me. At the time, hustle culture was booming, and there were pervading messages everywhere encouraging people to build online platforms and to know your niche, along with mounting pressure to establish yourself as a unique expert in your field. It wasn't long before the term *influencer* made its way into our vernacular. Meanwhile, I found myself longing to build a "bench," a safe space for my reader to rest. I wanted to sit alongside them instead of positioning myself above them on my platform as I spoke *at* them. I doubt this is an original thought, but it's how I've come to approach social media over the years.

I don't think I would have been nearly as successful had my primary motivation been to gain followers and fame. Don't get me wrong. Being able to write books has been one of the greatest privileges of my life, and I acknowledge that the publishing industry does leverage platforms for profit, but that isn't what got me to where I am today. Intentionality, obedience, and reverence for God's Word are what led me to write the posts that eventually put me on Britt's radar. It wasn't a strategy that caught her attention; it was my heartfelt sincerity.

There were plenty of painful rejections and redirections along the way that would have crushed me if I had built my foundation upon a desire for approval from others. Building a foundation on popularity and the opinions of others is like building a house on sand. It shifts whenever the tide comes in and comes crashing down when the rain falls and the wind blows. It doesn't hold firm when hard times come. Notice I said *when* and not *if*, because hardship eventually comes for us all.

There's an Old Testament prophet who knew a thing or two about experiencing the disapproval of others. Let's talk about Jeremiah. The prophet's obedience to God didn't exactly make him friends; his decision to proclaim the word of the Lord made him enemies in high places. In addition to experiencing the harsh judgment of others, Jeremiah also experienced cruel punishment. One incident takes place in Jeremiah 20, when Pashhur, the chief officer of the priests, takes it upon himself to have Jeremiah beaten and placed in the stocks, only released the next day, after suffering excruciating physical pain and public humiliation (vv. 3–5).

Jeremiah's obedience to God cost him dearly. He had to pay a painful price to remain faithful to his role as a messenger of God. As a matter of fact, Jeremiah considered either giving up or changing the message God had given to him on multiple occasions. He might not have said this publicly, but Jeremiah clearly wrestled with the tension of the suffering and humiliation he faced inwardly and openly with God. I imagine he wanted to quit and stop speaking out.

Have you ever considered giving up? I'll be the first to admit that I have, often. I'm not proud of the fact that I've danced with defeat, but it's true. I've told you I value honesty, and that starts with me. I think it's important to remember that our obedience to Christ will often come at a personal cost. For me, it's my comfort. This ultimately points to what I value most, which is safety and security. Following God is risky. Ask anyone who has dedicated their life to Jesus. The Old Testament prophet Jeremiah knew this better than most of us could possibly comprehend. But, ultimately, Jeremiah's trust and belief in God empowered him to press onward toward his calling.

I, too, have experienced obedience coming at a cost. I've lost friendships, social media followers, and opportunities because of my choice to be obedient to what I felt God was calling me to do. But when we choose faithfulness over fame, we change the game. The earthly rewards no longer satisfy and entice us. We no longer live our lives within the confines of other people's comfort zones. And as we choose to obey, God increases our capacity beyond what we could have done on our own.

Matthew 6:33 says, "Seek first his kingdom and his righteousness, and all these things will be given to you as well" (NIV). Matthew didn't say to seek health, wealth, popularity, and prosperity, and all these things will be given to you. No. He said to seek God's kingdom first. I know this is much easier to read than it is to live out. I've got years of experience fighting my own selfish ambitions, but I can tell you there is freedom found in seeking God first.

Following God will often come with adversity and opposition, just like it did for Jeremiah. It will not be easy, but it will be worth it. Just as Jeremiah chose to bring his pain and problems to God, we, too, need to make the intentional choice to go to God first. Prioritizing His kingdom above building our own.

This looks like constant surrender and placing our preferences at the foot of the cross. It looks like choosing faithfulness over fame.

Let's be faithful to the One who has always been faithful to us, no matter the cost.

REFLECTION QUESTIONS

1. Do you relate with the stories of David and Jeremiah? If so, in what way?
2. Do you struggle with seeking the approval of others more than you seek God?
3. What does your obedience to God cost you?
4. In what ways can you choose faithfulness to God today over the desire for fame and popularity?

THREE

THE LITTLE THINGS
DO MATTER

There's a poem in a delicate floating glass frame that sits on my (Cass's) kitchen counter, right between my ivy plant and the stove. I see it every day as I prepare our family's meals, but if I'm honest, it usually blends into the background of our busy life. Today, that wasn't the case. I'm not ashamed to admit I've been wrestling with depression and feeling lost in the hustle and bustle of the everyday. When life gets overwhelming, I'm tempted to view the blessings in my life as burdens. That definitely was the case for me today.

Frustration became my companion as I tried to pry sticky popsicle sticks off the counter. Mumbling and grumbling under my breath, I bent down to pick up dirty underwear off the bathroom floor—again. Secretly longing for a life of significance, in my heart I began to despise the small things. I rinsed the grit and grime off the dishes in our sink. *There's got to be more to life than this*, I was thinking when I glanced up and saw the poem sitting on my counter. I paused to notice the letters, each one carefully and intentionally typed onto the page.

This piece of paper was the only gift I asked for last Christmas. I'd been following the poet who wrote it, David Gate, on social media for a while, and his words often ministered to me. The fact that David types every single one of his poems himself adds a sentimental value for me personally. The typewriter font brought up fond memories of someone dear to me, Grandma Jan. I grew up visiting my grandma's apartment. Grandma Jan was my *person*, and I owe my adoration for the written word to her. She was my safe place, a refuge from the chaos of my childhood. Her apartment was the closest thing I'd ever seen to Belle's library from the movie *Beauty and the Beast*. My memory of my childhood is a bit foggy, so I might be remembering it as more grandiose than it actually was, but to me it was Disney princess–worthy. She had rows and rows of bookshelves, an antique writing desk, and a vintage typewriter.

I learned how to use Grandma Jan's typewriter early. I might have been six years old when I started writing on it. I could barely spell—to tell the truth, I still can't spell well—and yet, there I was, pouring out my heart onto piles and piles of pages of crisp white paper. I became obsessed with writing stories and scripts for plays that no one other than my grandma would read. That typewriter contains some of my fondest childhood memories. I think that's partly why David's poems stood out to me. His poetry was beautiful, yes, but the typewriter font called to me. I knew I had to have one of his poems in my home. And this is the one that now spoke to me from my kitchen counter:

> Doing the laundry
> and the dishes
> and meal preparation
> are not tasks of the mundane
> because being clothed
> and clean
> and fed
> declares the dignity
> of human life
> and nurtures us
> into new days
> into new eras
> they are not mundane, no
> they are the rituals of care.[1]

These words are a daily reminder to pause and remember that there's great purpose in what seems miniscule or mundane. That every moment can be holy and that nothing is truly mundane when done for God's glory.

Some days—maybe most days, for some of us—we do find ourselves elbow-deep in dishes, with the laundry pile giving us the side-eye and the to-do list practically laughing at us.

These sorts of days feel a million miles away from the grand stories we read about in those jaw-dropping testimonies. Yet, as David's typewritten poem reminds me, right there, in that ordinary yet remarkable moment, is an incredible opportunity to honor God.

What does that look like? You might be wondering, *How does my laundry time bring honor to God?* Bringing honor to God in our daily moments involves being conscious of Him in our routines, decisions, and interactions. We've created a list for you of some practical ways to honor God in the seemingly small moments of each day.

- **Prayerful Awareness.** Begin your day with prayer, inviting the Father to guide your thoughts, words, and actions throughout the day ahead. This sets a tone of reverence and awareness.
- **Saturation in the Word of God.** Take a few minutes every day to meditate on a specific passage of Scripture. This can be during a break, before meals, or even while commuting to and from where you need to go. Put it on repeat, sis!
- **Acting in Love.** Be the hands and feet of Jesus. Small acts of Christ's love like holding the door for someone, offering a word of godly encouragement, or simply telling someone that God loves them can be a reflection of His love.
- **Gratitude in the Mundane.** Even in daily tasks like doing dishes or driving to work, find something to be

thankful to the Father for. This attitude of gratitude turns mundane moments into worship.

- **Godly Integrity.** Make decisions, even minor ones, with integrity. Whether it's being honest about a mistake at work or choosing not to gossip, these moments reflect a heart that seeks to please God in all things.
- **Mindful Speech.** Aim to speak words that uplift, build up, encourage, and bring peace. Ephesians 4:29 advises, "Let no corrupting talk come out of your mouths, but only such as is good for building up, as fits the occasion, that it may give grace to those who hear."
- **Guarding Your Thoughts.** While it's natural to have a range of thoughts, be intentional about focusing on what's pure, lovely, and praiseworthy, as Philippians 4:8 suggests.
- **Remaining Humble.** Recognize that every moment, even the small ones, is an opportunity given by God. A humble heart is always ready to be molded, to learn, to grow, and to serve.
- **Being Teachable.** A teachable heart is the result of humility, but it's much more than that. Living with a willingness to admit you don't have the answers leads to seeking God and biblical truth. Commit yourself to accepting constructive correction, asking questions, gleaning from the wisdom of others, and being willing to repent and learn from mistakes. We can choose to view failure as a loss or a lesson (Proverbs 9:8–9).

These are all great ways to incorporate a heart seeking to honor God into your day-to-day activities. We personally like to pick one or two to focus on throughout a day so we can be more intentional with our time. Doing so has helped us view even the smallest of moments as sacred opportunities. You can try something similar and see how that changes your outlook!

Now, there is one more way we can honor God in our regular activities, and that is the act of stewardship. This one bears some digging into, so let's linger here together for a while. Being a good steward is an important role in the realm of micro purpose. Stewardship as a believer can be broken into three main categories: time, resources, and gifts.

So, how can we be good stewards of all three? Let's first take a look at time.

STEWARDING OUR TIME

It's important to keep in mind that time is something we don't get back. It is the one currency that is in limited supply; we only have so much of it here on earth. When we invest it properly, the return is rewarding. However, when we invest improperly, the return can be lacking.

Every second of our day is an opportunity. To genuinely trust God with the bigger picture, we need to find Him in the everyday, in the micro moments. Establishing these daily connections with Him by stewarding our time well ensures that our trust in His promises becomes unshakable.

However, let's be candid. In the context of today's society, distractions are at our fingertips all day, every day, making it a challenge to steward our time effectively. Pause and consider just how many precious moments have been spent mindlessly scrolling or binge-watching, or, if you're like me (Britt) in my latest iteration of time-wasting, playing games on my phone. Trust me, this was not my proudest moment. But after what felt like the millionth Facebook invite from my oldest brother, Ben, I gave in to curiosity (or was it sibling peer pressure?) and downloaded Monopoly Go! It was Monopoly but with a digital twist. I was expecting a nostalgic trip down Boardwalk and Park Place, but, instead, I landed on what felt like an addictive casino version of our beloved childhood game.

Here's the funny (or maybe not-so-funny) thing: I was initially baffled by the game. I didn't understand what the hype was all about. I thought I'd be engaging in strategic property trades with a friend one-on-one, but nope! It turned out to be more about rolling dice, accumulating virtual wealth, and getting those little "Congratulations!" pop-ups that feed the soul with dopamine hits like empty calories. Before I knew it, hours had vanished into thin air. Poof! All in pursuit of advancing my digital net worth and acquiring virtual properties. But let's face it, aside from giving me a strange sense of accomplishment (my net worth was nearly $3 billion, thank you very much), it added absolutely zero value to my life. It was the epitome of wasting time, wrapped up in a shiny, animated package.

So, what's the lesson here? Sometimes our leisure activities are more about mindless entertainment than actually rejuvenating our souls. It's like snacking on chips when you're not even hungry—momentarily satisfying but, ultimately, empty calories for the brain. This brings to mind the cautionary words from Ephesians 5:15–17: "Look carefully at how you walk, not as unwise but as wise, making the best use of the time, because the days are evil. Therefore do not be foolish, but understand what the will of the Lord is."

Is it wrong to have leisure activities? No. In fact, they can be quite refreshing and necessary. Is it wrong to waste hours upon days playing a game that adds absolutely no value to our lives? It might not be explicitly wrong in moderation, but does it draw me closer to Christ and aid me in fulfilling the purpose He has for me? That's the real question.

Consider this: Are you living life wisely, maximizing every opportunity? Are your actions in alignment with the will of the Lord?

I'll be the first to admit, I don't always maximize every opportunity. My actions haven't always been in alignment with what I feel is His will for my time. In fact, I've been a huge waster of time during certain seasons of my life. If leisure activities were a sport, I'd be a pro at it. I've wasted an entire decade being stagnant, and I've seen firsthand the damage that can come from that (zero out of ten, I don't recommend). More on that later. But I'm thankful that we love and serve a redeeming God who takes our mistakes and crafts something beautiful out of them. And I've certainly learned my lesson. How we allocate our time directly impacts our spiritual growth and the depth of our relationship with God. Every moment we choose to be available to Him is a testament to our commitment to Him as we honor His will for our lives.

Friend, our intent is not for you to read these words and hang your head in shame if you haven't made the most of your time. Rather, our hope is to emphasize the significance of your life, your role in the body, and every decision you make. You are important, and the body of Christ urgently needs you to step into where God is calling you right now.

By being good stewards of our time, we get to mirror Jesus' own intentionality during His ministry on earth. He prioritized moments of solitude and prayer, even during the pressing demands of His ministry. By following His example, we can ensure that our days are not just filled with activity but with purposeful actions that reflect a heart wholly devoted to God.

However, stewardship of time isn't just about what we choose to *do*; it's also about what we decide to *forgo*. And this is a hard one. But by setting boundaries, avoiding needless distractions, and being selective in our commitments, we create proper space and margin for God to work within and through us. That means turning down specific opportunities or activities that might pull us away from our primary mission, even if they seem reasonable in their own right. Sometimes opportunities can turn sour if entered into without His endorsement. That's not to say that God can't work out some good in our situation (Romans 8:28), but "some good" doesn't always mean "His best."

Being a good steward in the realm of micro purpose is about making conscious choices that reflect a heart desiring to honor God. It means recognizing that every second does count. No matter how big or small, every choice sends ripple effects. Minutes turn into hours, hours turn into days, days turn into weeks, weeks turn into months, and months turn into years. It all adds up, so we must consider how we spend our time.

> **STEWARDSHIP OF TIME ISN'T JUST ABOUT WHAT WE CHOOSE TO *DO*; IT'S ALSO ABOUT WHAT WE DECIDE TO *FORGO*.**

STEWARDING OUR RESOURCES

Now, let's turn our focus to a different aspect of stewardship, the intentional stewarding of all the resources God has entrusted to us. For instance, stewardship of resources can look like giving financial support to causes that are close to God's heart. This might mean giving to your church, a parachurch ministry, or a nonprofit. It could also mean sowing into a missionary or simply practicing generosity in your community. But stewarding your resources isn't always about money. Something as simple as making a double portion of a meal you're preparing to share with a sick friend can be faithful stewardship of your resources too.

Another way of stewarding your resources is simply being wise with them. I (Cass) have found a unique way to maximize what I have through something as simple as making homemade bone broth. Every time I buy a rotisserie chicken, my youngest daughter, Charlotte, and I make a project of it. She loves the process of helping me pull all the meat off the bones, chopping up vegetable scraps from leftovers, adding thyme, rosemary, and garlic into the slow cooker with the chicken bones, and storing the meat in a freezer bag for a meal later in the week. We let the concoction simmer for ten to twelve hours on low, and the finished result is a delicious, nutrient-dense broth we can use for future meals. Sometimes good stewardship is simply making something out of what might seem like a whole lot of nothing.

Matthew 6:21 echoes in my heart when I think about honoring God with our resources: "Where your treasure is, there your heart will be also." The concept of a person's treasure and heart being in the same location illustrates the fact that we invest in what matters most to us. But stewardship, as Jesus teaches us, isn't just about managing resources wisely. It's also about being aware of where we place our trust and allegiance, as we see in the Sermon on the Mount, one of the most well-known lessons Jesus taught (Matthew chapters 5–7). In this sermon, Jesus calls His disciples to an unwavering devotion to God and His kingdom, which will lead them to trust in God for all their needs rather than spending time worrying about what they have and don't have.

Let's break this down into language that is easier to digest. Our allegiance must be given to God and God's kingdom rather than to money or possessions. Seeking God's kingdom needs to be our highest priority. When we trust God with our resources, our tendency to worry about our daily needs lessens and we're able to instead take a bigger-picture point of view both on what and how much we can give to others and on how we use or maximize what we've been given. Matthew 6:25 drives this point home: "Therefore I tell you, do not worry about your life, what you will eat or drink; or about your body, what you will wear. Is life not more than food, and the body more than clothes?" (NIV).

You may be thinking, *Yes, I know that honoring God with my resources matters, but sometimes I'm just so scared that we won't have enough to live on.* The hard truth is when it comes to our resources, fear often gets in our way. This is where the difference between our professed beliefs and our functional faith matters.

Worry is a natural response to the reality of scarcity. But we also know that John 10:10 teaches us about abundant life. It's hard to keep that in mind when we feel the stress and strain that come with life on this side of heaven. So how do we trust God in the middle of, well, life? Trusting God is made possible through the supernatural power of the Holy Spirit. When we're able to focus on God's unwavering character in the face of uncertainty, we access an unexplainable peace that surpasses our understanding (Philippians 4:7). Trusting God with our anxieties is possible, despite the reality of scarcity.

I'll admit this is *really* difficult for me to live out. Just last summer, my relationship with money was put to the test. I was invited to attend Denver Seminary's first Women's Leadership Cohort to pursue a master of biblical and theological studies degree. At first, I didn't even consider applying because I didn't have a bachelor's degree, but then God removed that obstacle when I was informed I could apply for an undergraduate exemption. It took a lot of hard work and God's grace, but I managed to get accepted (What can't He do?!). But getting into seminary was only the first challenge. Then came the financial side of things.

The week before our courses began, I found out my husband's GI Bill benefits were no longer transferable to me unless he was to pass away (bummer), which meant, although my husband had earned the financial provision United States military members and their families get for college tuition through his time sacrificing and serving our country, because he didn't assign his benefits to me in 2016 when he left US Air Force active duty, those benefits were no longer available to me.

Hindsight truly is 20/20. We had no idea then that I'd be pursuing seminary today. This realization left me reeling and questioning everything. We were barely getting by already; did I really want to take out student loans and create more debt for our little family? I felt like perhaps I was reaching beyond my limitations and should accept it just wasn't meant to be. I experienced panic attacks each time I logged into my bank account app. I found myself struggling to trust God with what I had today because I was worried about tomorrow. I found myself looking up job listings, trying to find a way to make the financial strain feasible. I was turning over every rock, looking for a solution instead of trusting God's provision. Maybe you can relate? But then I received a significant discount on my tuition that, combined with a student loan, made the financial burden more manageable for our family, although it remains a substantial investment.

God made a way where we saw no way. He knew what we lacked, and He filled in the gap. This is what I was referring to earlier when we talked about our professed beliefs meeting functional faith. I really had to trust Him in this situation, knowing that if He called me to attend seminary, He would walk me through it. I had to place my treasure in Him, not in what I was lacking.

If you're uncertain if your treasure is in Jesus or in your resources, here are a few questions to ask yourself:

- Do I put my money and my resources where my trust is?
- Is the way I'm utilizing my resources aligning with what I say I believe about God?
- Do my actions align with my values? If not, what is one step I can take toward placing my resources in God's hands today?

I'm the first to admit, trusting God with our resources and stewarding them well is hard and holy, but doing so gives us access to peace that surpasses rationality. We know that our fear of scarcity and anxieties are part of our lived reality on this side of heaven. There will be times when we must trust God for our daily bread, literally. At least, that's been the case for me and my family, but God has *never* left us hungry. The question once again is this: Where is our treasure, and is it truly found in Him?

My life is living proof that when our treasure is in Christ, He alone sustains us. The same can be true for you. I believe there's financial peace ahead for you if you're willing to place your trust in Him. More than that, there's hope for every hopeless situation if we're willing to let go of our desire to find our own solutions and simply trust His provision. The Bible doesn't promise us we'll have everything we want, but it does remind us that God knows what we need. So rather than grasping too tightly what we've been given, let's loosen our grip and seek God for direction on how to steward it well.

Having explored how we can honor God with our resources, let's now shift our attention to the gifts He has given each of us (and you) and how we can use them for His glory.

STEWARDING THE GIFTS
GIVEN TO US BY GOD

There have been multiple seasons of each of our lives when we've squandered our gifts and talents. Not always deliberately. There are various reasons we ended up neglecting our spiritual gifts and God-given abilities. But, as a result, we both know what it's like to become stagnant, discouraged, and unmotivated.

I (Cass) remember when my family first moved to Oklahoma City. I was super excited to get involved with the women's ministry in our local faith community. If you read our first book, *Her True Worth*, you know that experience ended in rejection and frustration. I couldn't understand at the time that what I perceived as a no was actually a "not here" from God. The pain of not feeling accepted left me confused and discouraged. Honestly, talking about it today still hurts. I didn't know where I belonged or how to use the gifts God had given me, and I wasn't willing to put myself out there again. I was scared of being hurt, so I basically took my ball and went home. I decided I wasn't going to serve if they didn't want to include me the way I thought I should be included. I basically went to church but intentionally decided I wasn't going to show up in this community.

I recognize now I didn't receive that no with grace or maturity. I was allowing my wound to write the narrative of that story. But in hindsight, I can see that the "not here" I received then was actually an invitation to approach ministry differently. I'm the type of person who prefers comfort and predictability and can tend to want to stay where I understand how things work, so I had to have my preferences stripped from me.

Not long after God told me "not here," I attended my first

writing conference in Waco, Texas, and Britt slid into my DMs (not kidding). That same week, I learned the ins and outs of the publishing industry, how to acquire an agent, how to pitch to an acquisitions editor, and how to write a book proposal. Tell me that isn't God! I still get emotional when I think about it. What I thought was a rejection was a drastic redirection.

Friend, even a "no," "not here," or "not now" has God's kindness written all over it. Even rejection is wrapped in His mercy. And sometimes we think we may have the right setup to utilize our spiritual gifts, but then God has something else in mind.

> EVEN A "NO," "NOT HERE," OR "NOT NOW" HAS GOD'S KINDNESS WRITTEN ALL OVER IT.

UNDERSTANDING SPIRITUAL GIFTS

As we're learning to steward our gifts, let's talk a little more about what the Bible says about spiritual gifts. Spiritual gifts, as outlined in the Scriptures, are special abilities given to us by God for the edification of the church and to fulfill God's purposes in the world. There are two general categories: manifestations and ministry gifts.

Manifestations

First, let's talk about manifestations. When we accept Christ as our Lord and Savior, each Christian receives the "gift of the Holy Spirit" (Acts 2:38). This is one gift that has nine different ways or "manifestations" in which it is revealed. Think of it as a Swiss Army Knife—one gift with many functions that is revealed in nine different ways (1 Corinthians 12:7–10):

- **Word of Wisdom.** When God provides a person with wisdom, direction, or guidance in how to apply the knowledge He has about something.
- **Word of Knowledge.** Receiving revelation or knowledge from God that is humanly unexplainable. This can be information, insight, or understanding about something.
- **Faith.** Exceptional trust in God's promises, power, and presence, often manifested in difficult circumstances.
- **Healing.** Serving as a conduit for God's healing power, which can be physical, emotional, or spiritual.
- **Miracles.** Being used as a conduit by God to perform supernatural acts that glorify Him.
- **Prophecy.** Communicating a message from God to His people.
- **Discerning of Spirits.** The supernatural ability to perceive the spiritual reality in a situation, distinguishing between the Holy Spirit's influence and that of evil spirits.
- **Speaking in Tongues.** Speaking prayer and praise to God in a language unknown to the speaker as a sign for unbelievers.
- **Interpretation of Tongues.** Translating messages spoken in tongues to edify the church.

Ministry Gifts

Not only do we all have the gift of the Holy Spirit, manifested in various ways, but we each have a ministry gifting we can use to help further God's kingdom. These ministry gifts are mentioned in Scripture and are given to us "to equip the saints for the work of ministry" (Ephesians 4:12; Romans 12:6–8; Ephesians 4:7–13; 1 Corinthians 12:28):

- **Administration.** Organizing, directing, and implementing plans to lead others.
- **Exhortation.** Encouraging and lifting others up through words of comfort and consolation.
- **Service.** Offering support or assistance, often behind the scenes, in various ways.
- **Leadership.** Guiding and shepherding others with vision and direction.
- **Mercy.** Demonstrating great compassion and empathy, especially to those suffering or in need.
- **Apostleship.** Building community by bringing unity and balance to the mix.
- **Prophecy.** Bringing messages from God to people, speaking specific prophetic words necessary for edification, exhortation, and comfort; recognizing ministry gifts in others; giving others spiritual direction; alerting the body of Christ to danger in the spiritual battle, and more.
- **Evangelism.** Sharing the message of the good news of salvation through Jesus Christ to the unsaved.

- **Pastoring.** Tending to the flock, caring for and tending to mental, physical, and spiritual needs.
- **Teaching.** Having the ability to explain and apply God's Word effectively, leading to understanding and transformation.

We hope seeing these lists will help you identify where God may be calling you to serve. Remember, each of you has been given gifts from God so that you may serve.

I (Britt) remember the first time I came across the list of spiritual gifts in the Bible. I had a mixture of excitement and, honestly, a bit of confusion. It was like discovering a hidden treasure that had always been there, waiting for me. I felt this surge of encouragement, almost like a gentle nudge from the Holy Spirit, saying, "Hey, this is for you too." It stirred something deep within me, kindling a desire to dive in and start using whatever gift I had been given.

How do you know what your gifts are? There's a wonderful resource called the Spiritual Gift Inventory that we highly recommend.[2] It includes a test that will help you assess what your gifting might be. We also encourage you to evaluate your strengths by talking with trusted friends or family members about the gifts they see at work in your life. Oftentimes, others can more clearly see what comes naturally to you than you can.

How does God use our gifts? It's important we recognize

that spiritual gifts are given to us for the benefit of the body of believers, not for our individual benefit. The purpose of our spiritual gifts is to point others to the hope we have in Jesus, to motivate people to seek God, to be empowered to love one another well, and to encourage one another to live in a manner that is worthy of Christ.

For example, my (Cass's) husband, Dan, is a natural giver. He has the gift of serving and thrives when given the opportunity to pour into the lives of others through acts of service, mentorship, and generosity. Dan also has a strong suit in faith, and when we're walking through something hard, I often ask him if I can borrow his faith because his faith is immovable, while mine is much more fragile.

It's interesting when you think about how each of our gifts functions within the body of Christ. In one area where we might be weak, another person might have a particular strength to make up for our weakness. It's a beautiful, complementary exchange. And yet, even though we've got this incredible toolbox at our disposal, it often feels like we're either not using the tools correctly, or, in some cases, not using them at all. And the sad thing is there are many of us who might be sitting on these amazing, God-given abilities, unaware that we have them.

But here's the thing: like any talent or ability, our spiritual gifts need nurturing. They aren't just handed to us in perfect form, ready to be utilized without practice or understanding.

Any fitness guru will tell you that muscle needs regular and consistent exercise to grow stronger. Likewise, the more we use our gifts, the more attuned we become to His leading and the more effective we are in our service to Him and others.

In 1 Timothy 4:14, Paul told Timothy not to neglect the gift he was given. Phew, that's a pretty strong encouragement and heavy conviction. It also teaches us that, unfortunately, these gifts can be neglected, which implies they need our attention. They need to be stirred up, honed, and developed.

So, how do we do that? How do we take these seeds of gifting and cultivate them into something that edifies the church and, ultimately, brings God glory? Well, it starts with recognition. From the moment someone becomes a Christian, they're given the gift of the Holy Spirit and receive their own specific gifts. Recognize that you have a gift. You do! Then, steward it. Nurture it, grow it, use it in love and service.

God uses our giftings in an intentional way to shine His light into the world. We're vessels for His glory, like a lighthouse guiding people to Christ. We reflect His light like the moon reflects the light of the sun. In this way, we're not the source of our giftings but merely a conduit for the Holy Spirit. For this reason, all the honor and glory that come from using our gifts rightly belong to God.

Choosing not to operate within your gifting is like hiding your light under a bushel (Matthew 5:15–16). The repercussion of not using your gifts is the people in your sphere of influence—friends, family, coworkers, your neighborhood, and those within your local faith community—don't get the opportunity to experience the power of God at work within you and through you.

You are gifted in your own unique way. We really do believe that about you. More importantly, we truly believe in the mighty power of God at work within you and through you. And the body of Christ needs you to walk in all the fullness He has for you.

As we mentioned earlier, it's important to remember that the stewardship of our time, resources, and spiritual gifting is how we honor God in the micro. God's power has given you everything you need—right here, right now.

As you seek to walk in that fullness, to steward all you've been given to work with, ask yourself, *Am I putting my time, resources, and abilities where my heart is? Am I working as if everything is unto Him?* We want to challenge you to take an honest inventory of your life and reflect on whether you're wisely stewarding what God has given you. If prompted, take a moment to confess the areas in your life where you've neglected to honor God. Today's a good day to start fresh and reprioritize.

REFLECTION QUESTIONS

1. Have you ever mistaken the blessings in your life as burdens or found yourself despising the small things in your heart?

2. What is one way you can honor God today in the seemingly small?

3. The three categories of stewardship are: time, resources, and gifts. Which area of stewardship is a strength in your life, and which area needs attention?

4. Do you know what your gifts are? If not, we want to encourage you to explore this area of your spiritual formation.

FOUR

FAITHFULNESS OVER FLAWLESSNESS

You know those glistening puddles you see on the road far ahead of you on a hot day? They look so real, right? When I (Britt) was a little girl, I'd straddle my bike and pause as I gazed ahead at the "puddle" far in the distance. Then I'd hurry up and pedal as fast as I could to catch it. Have you ever done this? The puddles seem so inviting from afar! But every time, as I approached, they would vanish! I ran inside one summer afternoon, upset and crying to my mom that my puddle had disappeared. Come to find out, the puddle I had seen was a mirage. Mirages look promising from a distance, but the closer you get, the farther they move away. That's a lot like the way we chase perfection in our lives.

Perfection. It's a word that sounds so absolute, so

unattainable, and yet, so many of us secretly (or not so secretly) chase after it. When I was engaged to be married, I obsessed over making sure everything was bridal perfect. You best believe I pushed myself hard in pursuit of this goal. Dieting, exercising, bending over backward—all to fit into that perfect bride mold for the day. I meticulously arranged every detail, from the delicately applied makeup that concealed every one of my blemishes to the cascading curls that framed my face, to the breathtaking Vera Wang gown that seemed to capture my every Disney-princess dream. And every time even a single wisp of hair threatened my flawless face, I'd tenderly and carefully tuck it away, guarding my pristine bridal appearance.

But my husband-to-be hadn't been standing at the altar waiting for this perfect version of me. He'd simply been waiting for me, the authentic me. My husband might have said yes to an image of me that seemed flawless, but in truth, he committed to the genuine, flawed me. He wasn't expecting me to be perfect, and I wasn't expecting him to be perfect. He loved me for me, imperfections and all. So the next time you are tempted to chase perfection, please let this example remind you that you don't have to.

In our human understanding, which the Bible tells us not to lean on, we can easily fall into the perfection trap (Proverbs 3:5–6). When we seek flawlessness, we can end up immobilized. Waiting for things to be perfect could quite possibly lead you to wait for something that might not ever occur.

I'm reminded of the parable of the talents in Matthew 25

whenever I think of the crippling pursuit of flawlessness. In this parable, the servant who buried his talent seems to have done so out of fear. Perhaps he was waiting for the perfect investment opportunity, maybe one that was going to at least double his money, but in doing so, he missed the point entirely. His master didn't seek a perfect return but a faithful effort.

For me as a young bride, what *if* that single wisp of hair had ruined some makeup on my face, or what *if* my dress somehow got ruined? Would it have dictated whether my husband said yes? Of course not! Would it have deterred me from walking down the aisle? Sure, I would've been disappointed, but my resolve to marry him was unwavering, even if I had to wear a black trash bag. I know Ryan would've had the same answer.

Unfortunately, for some, any deviation from perfection can be a deviation from purpose. Let me say that again. When you become too fixated on perfection, any deviation from being able to show up as your perfect self can keep you from showing up at all. I have been this person time and time again. Maybe you have too? This pause, this hesitation in our journey, can derail us from the path God has set for us. Waiting for perfection can mean missed opportunities, unrealized potential, and, crucially, a heart that is not fully engaged in God's work. This type of waiting can also

> **WHEN YOU BECOME TOO FIXATED ON PERFECTION, ANY DEVIATION FROM BEING ABLE TO SHOW UP AS YOUR PERFECT SELF CAN KEEP YOU FROM SHOWING UP AT ALL.**

lead to not participating, even when we're right where God has called us to be.

EMBRACING IMPERFECTION

Have you ever seen a mosaic? This art form beautifully captures the essence of our lives in God's hands. It's created by assembling a myriad of broken and fragmented pieces. At first glance, you see the collective beauty, but upon closer inspection, you realize its allure comes from the imperfect, varied fragments brought together. Just like in a mosaic, our imperfections combined with God's artistry create a breathtaking masterpiece.

Often, we can't see the big picture. We focus on the imperfect fragments and start obsessing over that one particular broken piece, eventually giving way to perfectionism. I (Britt) have had lots of defining seasons in my life when perfectionism has gotten the best of me. One example that immediately comes to mind is when I became a mom.

Motherhood, with its beautiful highs and challenging lows, has presented a whole new arena of struggles to me. When my firstborn daughter came into this world, it was like an unseen weight of perfectionism settled onto my shoulders and gave me a heavy burden I hadn't had before, a burden I tend to still carry. The constant attempts to hit the impossible standards set around motherhood have been both draining and elusive. My daughter's nursery? It had to resemble those perfect, aesthetically pleasing nurseries you see all over social media. Her baby bottles? They needed to sparkle, devoid of even the tiniest smudge. If there was a smudge, fear would shout that *surely she'd get sick* or *it's riddled with bacteria*. From the way I folded her onesies to the precise manner I bathed her, everything had to align just so. If it deviated even a smidgen from my idea of perfection, a cloud of failure would hang over me. Sometimes I feel that even now.

I sometimes wonder if this is my way of grasping for control in a realm that still feels so foreign to me. Perhaps there's a bit of fear driving me as well? Maybe my trying to mold everything into a picture of perfection is in pursuit of a shield against the vulnerability and unpredictability of motherhood. But the weight of these expectations becomes a self-imposed prison. It feels sort of like I have trapped myself in a cage of unrealistic expectations. When I inevitably fail, I start to spiral.

I saw this in my journey with breastfeeding. I'd envisioned those serene moments when my newborn and I would bond in the quiet harmony of nursing. But the reality for me is that it wasn't a quiet harmony. My daughter's shallow latch meant each session was a toe-curling, painful experience, and I'd grip onto any ounce of strength I had just to endure it. Instead of those dreamy, pain-free moments I'd seen other moms experience, I battled through a storm of discomfort. Those struggles felt like daggers, piercing me with the sense that I was somehow lacking as my daughter's mommy.

In hindsight, I see how flawed my perspective has been. I

realize now that perfection truly isn't the measure of a mother's love or her capability. However, in the thick of the hard moments and in the depth of insecurities, these distortions can be all-consuming. It's so easy to blur the lines between wanting the best for our littles and tying our self-worth to unattainable standards.

The allure of perfection is hard to resist. It promises us admiration, respect, control, and perhaps even a sense of personal fulfillment. God values authenticity, a heart willing to be mended and used by the very hands that fashioned us. Once I'm willing to give myself permission to fail and to not show up perfectly, I'm then able to see His grace and strength woven into each aspect of motherhood.

A guiding principle for me personally, especially in the realm of motherhood, is this verse that I hold so near to my heart: "He said to me, 'My grace is sufficient for you, for my power is made perfect in weakness'" (2 Corinthians 12:9). God delights in using our weaknesses, so much that His strength is made perfect in our weakness. It's less about us and more about Him. We see this play out time and time again in the Bible.

Just look at the apostle Paul, who was instrumental in spreading Christianity. He didn't shy away from his shortcomings. Instead, he used them to demonstrate God's strength (2 Corinthians 12:1–10).

Then there's Jacob, who, after an intense encounter with God, was left with a limp. This mark, a physical reminder of his struggle, also stood as a testament to his encounter with the almighty God. It wasn't Jacob's strength but his vulnerability that brought him closer to God (Genesis 32).

Gideon is another beautiful example. Despite seeing himself as weak, God saw him as a mighty warrior. It was when Gideon put aside his self-doubt and embraced God's vision that he stepped into his purpose (Judges 6).

The pattern is clear: God's focus isn't on our perfection but on a heart yielded to Him.

We can't always be waiting for things to be perfect, waiting for the conditions to be "just right," before we step into God's plan. If we stand still, aiming for unreachable perfection, we'll be standing still for the foreseeable future. But if we step forward in faith and embrace each imperfection, we get to watch as God uses them for what He had planned all along.

Picture your life as that mosaic. Each experience, mistake, triumph, and tear are the pieces that God uses. Alone, they might not seem like much. But in His hands? They come together to tell a story of His grace, His mercy, His unfailing love, and His redemption through the cross.

"IF I'M NOT PERFECT, THEN I'M NOT SHOWING UP."

I (Britt) have found that art is an unexpected teacher in my battle against perfectionism. My experience as an artist has never been about creating photorealistic art. Though I deeply admire artists who can look at something and make an exact copy of it, I've never been gifted with that ability. Instead, I've found solace in the world of abstract impressionism. This style of art is characterized by an emphasis on the overall impression in the totality of the art versus precise detail. Abstract impressionism allows me to create fluidly with no rules and no perfectionism to attain or adhere to. There's no stringent plan or meticulous focus on exactness, just the freedom to express through the gift God has given me.

But when I was asked to create artwork for our devotional, *There's Beauty in Your Brokenness*, I felt overwhelmed. I doubted my qualifications as someone who had only been creating art for a few years. I felt like a clump of seaweed amid a sea of expertise. Advanced color theory and other nuances of art seemed like knowledge that would take years for me to learn, knowledge I didn't yet have as I approached this task. I remember asking myself, *Shouldn't I have, like, an art degree or something to do this?*

IF HE'S ASKING US TO DO SOMETHING THAT FEELS BEYOND OUR ABILITIES, HE MUST SEE SOMETHING IN US THAT WE HAVEN'T YET REALIZED IN OURSELVES.

But what does "being qualified enough" really mean when God entrusts us with a task? If He's asking us to do something that feels beyond our abilities, He must see something in us that we haven't yet realized in ourselves. Trusting that He knows the outcome, our role is simply to abide in Him.

As the process of creating art for this devotional began to unfold, I started biting my nails in anxiety, and self-doubt began to set in. Oh, hello again, perfectionism. I wish I could say it's nice to see you.

My workflow looked a lot like this:

> Creating → erasing → creating → doubting →
> deleting → creating → erasing → placing my
> iPad down in defeat and loudly sighing.

In my frustration, I felt a gentle nudge from the Holy Spirit, a whisper encouraging me to *let go and just create as an act of worship.*

There it was. I was called to create as an act of worship. Worship. Not something where I'm constantly worried about "getting everything right," just a simple act of offering my heart to God.

The beautiful silver lining in all this is that this struggle with perfectionism in my art has become a doorway to discovering how to worship my Creator with the talents He gave me. I'm learning a lesson in surrender, in offering my art back to God as a form of praise and devotion, despite the imperfections.

This experience brings to mind Ecclesiastes 11:4: "Whoever watches the wind will not plant; whoever looks at the clouds will not reap" (NIV). If we wait for the perfect conditions, we'll never get anything done. This kind of mindset keeps us from starting, trying, completing, and putting our gifts to good use as we get too caught up in the *what ifs* and the *not good enoughs*. It's almost like saying, "Unless I'm Steph Curry, then I'm never going to shoot a basketball even one time." It sounds hilarious, but the struggle is real, my friend! This is what we do. We say, "Unless I'm going to be the best or be perfect, I'm not even going to give it a shot."

In Scripture, we can see the church of Corinth was far from perfect. Yet, Paul didn't advise them to wait until they had everything sorted out. Instead, he encouraged them to grow, to act, and to engage with their faith, flaws and all.

This is the "come as you are" party, not the "wait until I get it all together," "I don't want to embarrass myself," or "what if I'm not the best?" party. Yet we make excuses upon excuses to delay ever doing what we know God is calling us to do because of one single reason: "If I'm not going to do it perfectly, I'm not going to do it at all."

Let's consider David in the Bible. Was he perfect? Far from it. He made significant, heartbreaking mistakes. Yet despite these imperfections, his heart's desire to seek God's will never wavered. We can see this in the words he wrote in the book of Psalms. Some were written in joy and praise, and some were written in heartbreak. Yet, God called him a man after His own heart (Acts 13:22). David's heart was set on God, even if his actions faltered. His willingness to turn back, repent, and strive forward was what set him apart.

Here's the beautiful thing, friend. God doesn't measure us by worldly standards of perfection. He has plans for us, not for a future time when we are flawless, but for right this very moment exactly as we are.

TAKING SPIRIT-LED RISKS

My (Cass's) husband and children love watching the movie *Evan Almighty* on repeat. It's a comedy about a successful news anchor turned congressman named Evan Baxter, who starts building an ark and becomes known as New York's Noah. There's a scene toward the end of the film when Evan's wife, Lucy, meets God at a diner while she's running away from her problems and her marriage. As you can imagine, Evan's project, as well as the random animals in sets of two that keep showing up everywhere he goes, has created chaos and strain on their family and their marriage. Lucy finds herself at a crossroads of sorts. Does she match her husband's faith and co-labor with him, or does she abandon the relationship entirely? Should she place her trust in an unseen God and come alongside her husband's mission, or will she jump ship and let Evan build the ark alone?

The scene widens, and we see her as the local news and surrounding patrons ruthlessly mock her husband. The camera then focuses on a man dressed in white, bussing tables. He's been in the background throughout the entire scene, but he hasn't been clearly within our view until now. The man makes a comment to Lucy about how much he's always loved the story of

Noah and mentions that he's a bit of a storyteller himself. This piques her interest and snaps Lucy out of her inner monologue. She's intrigued and surprised by this stranger's statement, and they strike up a conversation.

Although it appears the two have never met, they begin to speak as if they're old friends catching up. No longer able to hold in her anguish, she begins to unload all her burdens to this stranger, and he nods as he listens. His empathy is palpable as he responds to Lucy's despair with wisdom and invites her to consider that this wild experience could be a wonderful opportunity for her family to bond. He then mentions that when we ask God to make our family closer (an exact prayer request Lucy has made in solitude), God doesn't zap people with warm fuzzy feelings but offers them an opportunity to bond, ultimately answering their prayer. He then makes a poignant remark about how, when we ask God for patience, God doesn't simply grant us patience but gives us experiences that prompt us to be patient.

Startled by this man's words, Lucy comes to the decision that she should support her husband on his God-given mission. We see Lucy's basket is empty as she thanks the man for his kindness. He then tells her to enjoy her meal as he walks away. Confused, she looks down to see her basket of fish and fries miraculously refilled! Bewildered, she looks up again to find the man is nowhere to be found.

What can we learn from this scene in a silly movie? Well, for starters, often what God has called us to do in obedience won't make sense and might be scary. It might also seem way beyond our own imperfect abilities. Evan didn't magically know how to build an ark that would house every kind of animal, and his choice to submit to God and build the ark could have cost him his career, his marriage, and his family. But he obeyed anyway. After her encounter in the diner, Lucy chose to do the same. Secondly, God is faithful to provide everything we will need to sustain the work He has ordained us to do (2 Peter 1:3–8). We see this in the way He provides encouragement, perspective, and clarity to Lucy as she's wrestling with the situation. And we also see this as God supplies Evan with all the tools, resources, and animals he's going to need in order to complete his mission, often to poor Evan's shock and dismay. It's comical but oh so relatable!

It's my experience that God doesn't often share the blueprints He has for our lives, nor does He give us detailed instructions like He did in the movie, though it would be awesome if that were the case! This is all movie magic, but it's not outlandish to say that God does indeed provide us with the things we'll need in order to do the work He has for us. Our choice is simply between giving way to fear about our own inadequacies and imperfections or having faith and obeying.

Faith and fear both ask us to place our trust in an unknown possibility. Both convince us of a certainty, either positive or negative, that we can't guarantee. We must decide which one we will place our trust in. Fear is intended to be a guard against danger. A healthy amount can be helpful in keeping us safe, like my five-year-old son's fear of heights. Too much fear, though, can rob us of our ability to learn valuable lessons and convince us that a leap of faith is far too dangerous.

In *Evan Almighty*, Evan and Lucy were both clearly freaked out by everything God was doing. Wouldn't you be a bit spooked if animals randomly appeared at your place of work and followed you around? They were understandably scared, but they didn't allow their fear to displace their faith. That's what being courageous is: acknowledging your valid fear and choosing to confront it anyway.

God tells us, "Do not be afraid" (Deuteronomy 31:6 NIV), but He never tells us our fear is invalid. The world can be a scary place, particularly when you consider the very real powers of principalities and darkness at play within the unseen realm (Ephesians 6:12). But being afraid isn't the problem; distrust and disobedience are. Fear can be a helpful guide at times, but it makes for a horrible boss. Don't let your fear be the boss of you! Feel what you feel, but don't allow your feelings and fear to speak louder than the voice of God. Put your fear in its place, friend.

USING WHAT YOU HAVE

Now that fear is in its rightful place, let's talk about another way inadequacy can show up and hold us back from taking steps toward our purpose: feeling disqualified. Let's begin by defining the word *disqualify*.

disqualify: (verb)

1. to deprive of the required qualities, properties, or conditions: make unfit
2. to deprive of a power, right, or privilege
3. to make ineligible for a prize or for further competition because of violations of the rules[1]

The Bible is full of stories of the least likely, lowly, and ineligible being chosen by God to bring Him glory. If we're being honest, we've both wrestled with the worry that we've been unfit and ill-equipped to serve God during multiple seasons of our lives. The truth is, we've both sinned against God, and those decisions should have made us ineligible for the ministry, but God's love covers a multitude of sins. The Enemy wants you to believe that it's your goodness that qualifies you for the call God has placed upon you, but that simply isn't true. Thankfully, it's not our own righteousness that qualifies us but rather Christ crucified who equips and empowers us.

In Paul's letter to the Roman church, he wrote:

All have sinned and fall short of the glory of God, and all are justified freely by his grace through the redemption that came by Christ Jesus. God presented Christ as a sacrifice of atonement, through the shedding of his blood—to be received by faith. He did this to demonstrate his righteousness, because in his forbearance he had left the sins committed beforehand unpunished—he did it to demonstrate his righteousness at the present time, so as to be just and the one who justifies those who have faith in Jesus. (Romans 3:23–26 NIV)

You might feel like you don't have what it takes to be used by God. Girl, we've got news for you! If you're willing, He is able. All you need to do is use what you have. Let's discuss three women who saw beyond the things the world would have used to disqualify them and used what they had, right where they were, to glorify God.

The Woman with the Alabaster Box

The woman with the alabaster box showed up at a dinner party with Jesus and some Pharisees, smashed the alabaster box of fragrant oil, and washed Jesus' feet with her tear-soaked hair. Some biblical scholars claim this could have been Mary Magdalene, but there's no evidence to support this theory. In John 12:3, Mary of Bethany also anointed Jesus' feet with aromatic oil, but that was a totally separate incident. One thing we know for certain is that, while this woman's identity is unknown to us, she was deeply known by God and we're still telling her story thousands of years later.

Think about this scenario. It'd be something if it happened today. But in biblical times, to say this behavior was wild would be a complete understatement. This would have been culturally unacceptable behavior for a man, but it was punishable behavior for a woman, and definitely unpardonable for a woman of her reputation. (Luke 7:37 NIV says the woman was known to have a *sinful* reputation, a code word for scandalous.) This unnamed woman knew the risk of what she was doing in crashing this powerful man's dinner party. She counted the cost, and she decided getting close to Jesus was worth the danger. Her bold profession of love and adoration could have cost her everything, but Jesus was worth everything she had.

The party was full of religious men who knew her reputation. Her presence in this Pharisee's home defied the religious elite and required tenacious faith. Surrounded by her accusers, she dared to approach Jesus. I imagine her with her head hung low, carrying the most valuable thing that belonged to her, painfully aware of her brokenness as she burst open the alabaster box of expensive perfume. Overcome by emotion, she knelt before Jesus, weeping, wetting His feet with her tears. Then she wiped them with her hair, kissed them repeatedly, and poured perfume on them (Luke 7:38). But that's not where the story ends.

The gathering was hosted by a Pharisee named Simon, who was curious about Jesus yet suspicious of Him. When Jesus arrived earlier that night, Simon didn't greet Him with a customary kiss. He didn't anoint Jesus' head with oil or offer Jesus any water to wash His feet. Simon's behavior was an intentional diss in this context—and Jesus called out Simon's disrespect by contrasting his behavior with the sinful woman's selfless act of courage.

When Simon saw the unnamed woman's intimate act of worship, he thought to himself, *If this man were a prophet, he would know who is touching him and what kind of woman she is—that she is a sinner.* And Jesus, knowing Simon's inward thoughts, immediately answered him, "Simon, I have something to say to you" (Luke 7:39–40). Let's take a moment to unpack this scene. This Pharisee goes from hosting Jesus to questioning Him in an instant, because he thought Jesus was incapable of seeing this woman's heart. In the following verses, when Jesus shares the parable of the two debtors (Luke 7:41–43), He clearly demonstrates He is able to read the human heart as He exposes Simon's inward monologue and his posture of self-righteousness. Next, we see a striking contrast when Jesus applies the parable to both Simon and the sinful woman (Luke 7:44–47). In doing so, Jesus teaches us that the more aware we are of our own desperate need for forgiveness, the more lavishly we will love.

Placing emphasis on the fact that the Pharisee was the one who couldn't see the woman clearly, Jesus challenged this man's judgmental thoughts, asking, "Do you see this woman, or do you simply see her sin?" Jesus saw a repentant heart where Simon could see only shame. It's important to note that the key to her forgiveness wasn't her love for Jesus but rather her faith in Him. God's Word says that we are saved by grace through faith in Christ Jesus and not by our own efforts or works (Ephesians 2:8–9). Meanwhile, the devil is our accuser. Like the Pharisee in Luke 7, he calls us by our sins, but God sees His Son and what He has done when He looks at us. In Christ, we're a new creation, redeemed and set free from our secret shame (2 Corinthians 5:17).

The woman in Luke 7 knew she couldn't avoid her brokenness if she wanted to access the wholeness found only in Christ. She knew that people might dismiss her, judge her, and misunderstand her, but they'd never hold the power to define her. Jesus was worthy of everything she had, including her life. Remember this truth: When you are at your lowest, when you feel like you are broken beyond repair, Jesus is there to put you back together. It's only when you are intimately aware of your need for forgiveness and choose to embrace your brokenness that you are able to experience the fullness of His love.

Jael and the Tent Peg That Won a War

Sometimes the gift in your grasp is found in an unexpected place. Take the story of Jael in Judges 4:17–22, for instance. She wasn't an Israelite, but she possessed a fear and reverence for the God of the Israelites that led her to lure their enemy to his death.

Let's dive into the scripture, shall we?

After losing a gruesome battle against the Israelites, the Canaanites' lead commander, Sisera, fled on foot and found himself at the tent of a Kenite woman named Jael. When Jael saw Sisera approaching, she welcomed him into her tent, saying, "Come, my lord, come right in. Don't be afraid" (Judges 4:18 NIV). Sisera likely did so without hesitation because he had reason to believe he would be harbored in safety, due to the alliance between Jabin, King of Hazor, and Jael's husband's family. Jael covered him with a blanket and gave him a drink of milk. After making himself comfortable, he instructed Jael to guard

71

the entrance while he rested and to say no if anyone asked if someone was there with her. But once Sisera was fast asleep, Jael picked up a tent peg and a hammer. Quietly, she approached him and then, with swift intentionality, "she drove the peg through his temple into the ground, and he died" (Judges 4:21 NIV).

There are so many historical and cultural dynamics at play in this story. For starters, Jael was a Kenite woman, a married woman for that matter. In her culture and time, women had the responsibility of setting up and tearing down the tents. This is an important fact that we'll revisit soon. Secondly, the people of the Old Testament understood hospitality as a biblical mandate from God. Jael wasn't an Israelite and didn't share their religious beliefs, but she would have been likely to abide by cultural norms when it came to hospitality. It's important to note that the hospitality of those days demanded you protect your guest as your own family and, in some cases, above your own well-being. To allow harm to come to someone you were hosting would have been considered shameful and ungodly behavior.

With this historical and cultural context in mind, the story of Jael is even more striking. Many scholars argue about what exactly transpired in Jael's tent to cause her to take such a severe and violent course of action against the Canaanites' lead commander. Some say she was physically harmed by him, while others say she was simply annoyed with his intrusive presence.

Although the details of this story are widely speculated, one thing we know for sure is that whatever took place in that tent was the beginning of a domino effect that would ultimately bring the Israelites victory in a war against their enemies. God had promised to deliver Sisera into the hand of a woman (Judges 4:9), but it wasn't the woman most readers would have anticipated. It would be natural to assume that victory would be delivered through the mighty judge of Israel, Deborah, but God has a tendency to deliver His promises through the least likely and the lowly. Jael lacked the power and privilege allotted to Deborah, but God was with her.

Remember when I shared how it was customary for women to have the tedious task of setting up and tearing down the tents? Well, a lifetime of pulling up and driving tent pegs was exactly the skill set God intended to use to fulfill His promise to destroy the Israelites' enemy. Often, what might look like a disadvantage can become our greatest asset. God used the wife of a Kenite to accomplish Sisera's end, and all He needed was the tent peg she had in her hand.

Rahab the Canaanite Prostitute in Christ's Lineage (Joshua 2–6 and Hebrews 11)

When, starting with Jericho, the Israelites were getting ready to claim the land that God had promised to them, their leader, Joshua, decided to send two spies into the city. When the spies arrived, they entered the house of a prostitute named Rahab and stayed with her. The king of Jericho heard that the Israelites came to spy on the land and sent a message to Rahab, saying, "Bring out the men who came to you and entered your house" (Joshua 2:3 NIV). But she chose to hide the men under stalks of flax on her roof instead.

Rahab knew the God of the Israelites had given them this land and begged the spies to swear by the Lord that because she decided to show kindness to them they would show kindness to her family when they came back to take the city. "Our lives for your lives!" the men assured her, saying, "If you don't tell what we are doing, we will treat you kindly and faithfully when the LORD gives us the land" (v. 14 NIV). Rahab agreed and eventually helped them escape by sending them down a rope from the window. The men instructed her to tie that same rope—it was red, so it was easily identifiable—in the window when the Israelites returned, and all those in the house with her would be spared. And that's exactly what happened (Joshua 2:12–24).

The book of Hebrews also makes reference to Rahab's act of radical faith in the face of danger:

> By faith the prostitute Rahab, because she welcomed the spies, was not killed with those who were disobedient. (Hebrews 11:30–31 NIV)

And here's the most amazing part of the story. Not only were Rahab and her family saved, but, if you look at the genealogy of Jesus, you'll see that she is named as the great-great grandmother of King David and that her line led to Jesus Himself (Matthew 1:1–17). Rahab was a known prostitute, and her home was likely considered a brothel. Isn't it fascinating that God was able to secure safety for His people in a den of sin? That even a breeding ground for despicable acts could be a refuge for God's use? And, furthermore, that God would one day choose to cohabitate with humanity through a descendant of Rahab? How magnificent is God's intentionality that He'd choose to use a nonbelieving Gentile with a scandalous reputation to bear the fruit of her womb and eventually fulfill His mighty plan for the redemption of all sin!

The stories of the woman with the alabaster box, Jael, and Rahab remind us that God delights in utilizing those the world would otherwise disqualify. The Enemy wants you to believe that God can't use you, that you don't have anything to offer, but that's simply not true. God can use what the world would consider useless for His glorious purpose. We're not sure what's been spoken over you or what odds might be stacked against you today, but here's what we do know: God is willing and able to do a mighty work within and through you, with whatever you have, imperfect though it may be, if you're willing to allow Him to. So the question is, what do you have that you can offer to the Lord?

The woman in Luke 7 had an alabaster box of fragrant oil that she used to worship Jesus, teaching us that those who know their desperate need love lavishly and are forgiven generously, while those who live in denial of their sin miss the point entirely.

Jael had a tent peg. Her culture wouldn't have considered her to be a woman with privilege or power, but God saw an opportunity to fulfill His promise and deliver the Israelites' enemy through her.

Rahab had her home. Where others saw a den of sin, God saw the solution to seize the land He had promised the Israelites. As a war was waging beyond the walls of Rahab's dwelling, God had already decided He would dwell among His people in the flesh, proving once and for all that sin would no longer hold the power to separate His people from Him.

Adequacy is like one of those Magic Eye books I used to check out from the library as a kid. It's an illusion. It's only when we pause, reorient our gaze, and fix our eyes on Jesus that the image becomes clear. The picture within the picture is suddenly within our view, but somehow we couldn't see it before. Adequacy can only be discovered when we remove all the other qualifiers distracting us and distorting our view. Remember, perfection isn't a prerequisite for walking in purpose.

The world might not see the value of what God has given you, but God's grace truly is sufficient for you. If what you're being called to do feels beyond you, maybe it is. But we've got good news for you: When God equips you, He empowers you. People can't disqualify you from what God has commissioned you to do. When you feel like your qualifications are called into question, walk in the power of the God who uniquely and specifically called you. All you need is what God's already given you. Take a moment to look at your life. What's currently available to you?

PEOPLE CAN'T DISQUALIFY YOU FROM WHAT GOD HAS COMMISSIONED YOU TO DO.

REFLECTION QUESTIONS

1. How does it make you feel to read that God's grace is sufficient for you and His strength is made perfect in weakness (2 Corinthians 12:9)?
2. Is fear the boss of you?
3. Do you feel disqualified from being used by God? Why or why not?
4. Was there a story we shared that deeply resonated with you? Which one? Why?

FIVE

CAN I REALLY
DO THIS?

I (Cass) have the immense privilege of mentoring a handful of women in their early twenties. I personally believe the years between the ages of twenty and thirty are significant years for making decisions. The decisions we make in that span of time influence the trajectory of the rest of our lives. Each of the women I mentor entered my life at a different stage in their own life, and all these women are currently transitioning into new seasons. Some are college graduates, working full time and navigating homeownership. Others are happily married and considering starting a family. And others are finishing school and figuring out what's next.

I've had the honor of watching these young women grow into mighty women of valor. As I've walked alongside them, they've sat on my couch and sifted through their hopes, fears, and uncertainties—especially when it comes to what God is calling them to do with their lives.

Here are some of the questions these women and others have asked about their calling:

- Where is a woman's place within the body of Christ?
- Is this my call or my pride?
- Am I interested in making myself known, or am I motivated by the goal to make God known?
- Am I overstepping the boundaries of Scripture to pursue this calling?
- Is this next step I'm considering a societal expectation or a biblical mandate?
- Am I incapable or disqualified from communicating biblical truth because I'm a woman?
- Does my ability to lead contradict the biblical standard of humility and meekness?
- Can I actually do this?

I get it, these are some heavy questions. And the Enemy takes these valid questions and sows confusion and frustration into an already tense topic. I'm not going to pretend I have all the answers to these questions, but I do have something to share that I think will help us shift our perspective when it comes to calling.

What do you think your calling is? I've heard women say,

"I'm called to be a wife/mother/entrepreneur/worship leader/ doctor/missionary/breadwinner/foster parent/homemaker." You fill in the blank. The list goes on and on. Although those statements might be true, and we'll get into pursuing those more specific and personal callings a little later, I think we too often miss the primary call mandated for all believers: the Great Commission.

What is the Great Commission? The Great Commission is Jesus' parting command in Matthew 28 to the disciples to go and make disciples:

> Go and make disciples of all nations, baptizing them in the name of the Father and of the Son and of the Holy Spirit, and teaching them to obey everything I have commanded you. And surely I am with you always, to the very end of the age. (Matthew 28:19–20 NIV)

The word *disciple*, which is *mathetes* in Greek, is translated to "pupil" and "follower," as in "go and make followers of Jesus." What does it look like to follow this call practically?

- **Know God.** Can you imagine trying to introduce a friend to someone you've never actually met yourself? Talk about awkward. For us to make followers of Jesus, we need to be following Him daily ourselves. It would be difficult to take someone somewhere we've never been. Likewise, our relationship with God equips and empowers us to share the gospel with others. Jesus said: "I am the way and the truth and the life. No one comes to the Father except through me" (John 14:6 NIV).

- **Be Known by God.** To be known by God is to be loved and adopted into the family of God. The apostle Paul described our being known by God in this way: "If anyone loves God, he is known by God" (1 Corinthians 8:3). The Old Testament prophet Jeremiah reminds us that God knew us even before He knit us together in our mothers' wombs (Jeremiah 1:5). It's hard to fully comprehend the depth of God's knowledge of us. He knows where we've been, what we've done, and yet He loves us. But this all sounds like something we can't actively pursue. How can we proactively be known? Being known by God, in the simplest of terms, looks like doing life with God. A book I'd recommend on the topic of living life with God is *With: Reimagining the Way You Relate to God,* written by Skye Jethani. I read it in seminary, and it truly reshaped my relationship *with* God. Pun intended.

- **Make God Known.** When Jesus told the disciples to go and make disciples of all the nations (Matthew 28:19–20), He wasn't looking for a one-time conversion to Christianity, although it does begin with a decision to follow Christ. Ultimately, He wanted the disciples to teach others what it looks like to dedicate their lives to Jesus daily. Disciples are formed through thoughtful and intentional demonstration, not through a one-time decision. They require guidance, much like children do. I'm not sure about you, but I require gentle correction and guidance too. This is why discipleship is much more than simply teaching the Word of God. It is also living it out together. For those of us who have family and friends who aren't believers, our lives will speak louder than any sermon we will ever preach. Be mindful that your life is making God known to those around you, and that you're living a life on mission.

You might be wondering, *What does the Great Commission have to do with answering the questions so many women have about purpose and calling? Especially within the body of believers?* Great question. I'm so glad you asked. Let's connect the dots together, shall we?

It's important that we first recognize that the Great Commission is gender inclusive. We see this truth demonstrated in the Gospels, where Jesus' heart toward women is revealed through his countercultural interactions with women of his time. Mary J. Evans, author of *Woman in the Bible*, noted, "[Jesus'] approach can accurately be described as revolutionary, and we must take care in assessing the impact of Jesus' approach from our 'post-revolution' standpoint, not to forget just how revolutionary it was."[1]

In a historical period that saw women as merely an extension of men, Jesus viewed women as invaluable members of God's family. Women were often living on the social margins back then, subjugated and subordinated, but the Gospels demonstrate Jesus' attitude toward women to be one of inclusion, discipleship, and protection. In His interactions with women of various ages, ethnic backgrounds, and socioeconomic conditions, Jesus not only made space for them, but He also intentionally invested in them by welcoming them as His disciples.

We see this happen throughout Jesus' ministry, but one instance stands out to me: the story of two sisters (Luke 10:38–42). When Jesus and His disciples came to their village, Martha and Mary invited them into their home. Martha was busy with her many hosting tasks, as she offered care through acts of service, while Mary sat at Jesus' feet and received care by attentively listening to Him. Both postures are valuable, but Jesus pointed out that listening to and receiving from Him is of higher priority than simply doing things for Him. Luke 10:42 says, "Mary has made the right choice, and it will not be taken away from her" (CSB). This interaction demonstrated the importance Jesus placed on discipleship being not just for the men but for the women as well. He didn't disqualify Mary; He praised her teachable spirit and priorities.

Throughout the Gospels, Jesus took a heart posture toward women that was without cultural restrictions and societal barriers. We see this truth further illustrated in the story of the Samaritan woman in John 4. While His disciples went into town to buy food, Jesus sat down near the local well and ended up having a private conversation with the woman who came to draw water. This was a woman others would have considered unclean. People of Jesus' time and culture would have viewed her as someone to be avoided at all costs, yet He saw her as someone worthy of conversation no matter the cost. Jesus rejected the societal prohibitions that would have separated Him from those He came to save.

But you know what's the most amazing part of the story? During their conversation, Jesus revealed Himself to her as the Messiah, something He'd never done up until that point. Then, in a stroke of divine irony, this woman became the OG evangelist! After Jesus disclosed His identity to her as the coming Christ, she wasted no time spreading the word far and wide. "Many of the Samaritans from that town believed in him because of the woman's testimony, 'He told me everything I ever did'" (John 4:39 NIV). Others may have seen her as unworthy of even speaking to, but Jesus saw her as someone to be included in His earthly ministry.

There is a place for women within God's Great Commission, yet the topic of a woman's place continues to be a widely debated issue within various denominations of Christianity. It's been a point of contention since the beginning, and perhaps it always will be.

A WOMAN'S PLACE

In our first book, *Her True Worth*, we talk about learning to live from the inherent worth found in Christ instead of living to obtain it. In this book, we desire to teach you how to live commissioned by Christ instead of looking for permission from other people. The questions posed in the previous section are a great example of this relentless pursuit of permission. We ask them because we're not sure we have permission to live on mission, and often our greatest hesitation is found in feeling unsure if we're even allowed to do things within the church. The answer to these overarching questions? Well, it depends on the faith community you're in.

As we dig into this issue, let's define some important terms:[2]

complementarianism (noun):
1. belief that men and women are created equal in their being, value, and personhood, yet they complement each other with different roles and responsibilities as manifested in marriage, family life, and in the church.[3]

In simple terms: Men and women are equal in personhood but not in function.

egalitarianism (noun):
1. a belief in human equality, especially with respect to social, political, and economic affairs
2. a social philosophy advocating the removal of inequalities among people
3. belief that men and women are created equal in their being, value, personhood, and function.[4]

In simple terms: Men and women are equal in personhood *and* in function.

These dueling schools of thought contribute to the immense confusion and division we as Christians experience when navigating the issue of a woman's place within the body of believers. They create and remove boundaries that dictate a woman's role and potential functionality. I (Cass) personally respect and learn from godly people who adhere to both sides of this theological spectrum. I think it's important to acknowledge the reality of these different theologies, because it helps us understand more fully the challenges we, as women of faith, face.

As a woman in full-time ministry, this can be a tricky tension for me. I've been invited to preach and teach in different capacities at both complementarian and egalitarian churches across the country. I've also been confronted with hostility in my local church lobby by an angry man simply because I have the audacity to be a woman in ministry. I've had scriptures thrown at me (out of context) and insults hurled at me by strangers on the internet. If this sounds outlandish to you, please know I'm not exaggerating. There are people who truly believe that women should be seen and not heard. For many women, this is our unfortunate reality, but I've got news for you: Our purpose as women of God isn't defined by *people.*

Here's the deal. The Bible makes it clear that women are seen and heard by God and He values their voices and contributions to the kingdom. Jesus deeply loves women. The words written in the New Testament are woven with this truth.

Let's take a look at Romans 16:1–16. I won't put the entire scripture reference here, as it's rather long, but, essentially, it's a list of people Paul sends greetings to within the church, many of whom are women. Please feel free to open your Bible or use your favorite Bible app and read along with me.

According to Michael F. Bird, in his commentary on the book of Romans:

> Several women are named, and their work noted by Paul including Phoebe: deacon, benefactor (Romans 16:1–2). Priscilla: co-worker, church planter, teacher, fellow-prisoner (Romans 16:3–5). Mary: works hard for others (Romans 16:6). Junia: missionary-apostle (Romans 16:7). Tryphena, Tryphosa, and Persis: women who work hard in the Lord (Romans 16:12). Mother of Rufus: mothering care for others (Romans 16:13).[5]

Here's why the women shouted out in this list are interesting. There are roughly 3,100 names mentioned in the Bible, 2,900 of whom are men with only 170 of the total being women.[6] Many of these few women who are named are the ones being praised by Paul in this letter to the Roman church. Paul clearly recognized the invaluable contribution of women and noted their necessity in serving the body of Christ.

Let's look at just a few of them. There's Junia, whom Paul calls "outstanding among the apostles" (Romans 16:7 NIV). Even the fact that Junia was identified as an apostle is a pretty big deal—not only historically but also within our current cultural context—much less that he considered her outstanding! I learned in my New Testament and Revelation course during the summer intensive that Junia's name was changed in multiple Bible translations to Junias, which wasn't a historical or cultural name in existence in first-century Palestine or in the Greco-Roman world. The name change apparently was made in an attempt to remove her femininity and make her appear to have been a male apostle.

As for our girl Phoebe, I have a feeling that Paul didn't have arts and crafts in mind when he sent her to Rome. Don't get me wrong. I love glitter and hot-glue guns as much as the next gal, but I don't think that was the type of work Paul gave her. Phoebe was a deacon of the church in Cenchreae. She was considered a woman of means, and she was the one tasked with the delivery of Paul's letter. Tom Wright said that, when it came to delivering this letter to the Romans, "Paul entrusted that letter to a 'deacon' called Phoebe whose work was taking her to Rome. The letter-bearer would normally be the one to read it out to the recipients and explain its contents. The first expositor of Paul's greatest letter was an ordained traveling businesswoman."[7] How amazing is that?

You know what else is interesting about women in the Bible? Women funded the ministry of Jesus. Let that sink in for a moment. In a society where women were viewed as second-class citizens, in a Greco-Roman culture (Israel was occupied by Rome) where women were viewed as deformed men,[8] and in a historical context where women and their bodies were considered men's property, a commodity to be traded and bartered for political power and financial gain, these women not only wielded substantial financial wealth but also invested it generously into Jesus' earthly ministry.

Luke mentioned multiple women Jesus healed who dedicated themselves to following and providing for Him (Luke 8:2–3), including Mary Magdalene and Joanna. One is thought to have offered provision through the wealth of her husband, while the other is thought to have supported Him through her high position in society. Regardless of the means with which these women poured into the work of Jesus, they both came with extraordinary risk and eternal reward.

Need more examples of women in the Bible who faithfully lived on mission? Here are just a few:

- **Deborah** was a military heroine and the only female judge of Israel in the Old Testament. She was chosen intentionally by God, not as a last resort but for this specific purpose.
- **Jael**, whom we talked about earlier, took down Sisera, the Canaanite commander of King Jabin. She used what she had in her hand and won a war.
- **Anna** was a Jewish prophetess who prophesied about Jesus at the temple of Jerusalem.
- **Priscilla and Aquila** became two of Paul's most valued associates, who "risked their necks for my life," according

to Paul's testimony in Romans 16:3–4. This husband-and-wife team became powerful church leaders in the book of Acts.

- **Mary Magdalene** is believed by many scholars to be the first apostle ever recorded. Some call her the "apostle to the apostles," because she was among the women sent back to the disciples to tell them Christ had risen. Of course, they didn't believe her at first, because a woman's testimony wasn't considered trustworthy in first-century Palestine. With this in mind, isn't it fascinating that Jesus chose to reveal Himself as the risen Messiah for the first time to a woman and instructed her to "go and tell"? This is just one of many examples of what is called "the Great Reversal," in reference to how the kingdom of God confounds and confronts everything we know on this side of heaven.

This isn't an exhaustive list of women throughout the Bible, but it's a great place to start. Some of these women's stories we're familiar with; others we've already mentioned in previous chapters or we're going to discuss throughout the rest of this book. And yet there are many other women whose names we may never know but whose stories are still being told thousands of years after their lives on earth came to an end.

These women, who faithfully lived a life on mission for God, likely felt uncertain, unqualified, and inadequate, just like we so often do. They faced historical and cultural barriers

READY AS YOU ARE

THERE'S MORE THAN JUST "ROOM FOR YOU" IN THE KINGDOM OF GOD; THERE'S A NEED FOR YOU. that made living on mission difficult and, in some cases, potentially deadly, but they didn't allow their obstacles to deter them. They were ready and highly capable, because God was with them. And I've got news for you: He's with you too.

So where is a woman's place within the body of Christ? Answer: A woman's place is wherever God has called her to be.

Sister, if you read nothing else we write in this chapter, we hope you read this and take it to heart: There's more than just "room for you" in the kingdom of God; there's a need for you. You're worthy of the space you take up within the body of Christ. Not by your own merit, but by the power and authority of God within you and through you. You don't have to wait for someone to approve of you or invite you to live on mission for God. The Great Commission is the only permission slip you need. Jesus is enough. Rest in this truth: He qualifies, equips, and empowers you to do the hard and holy work He's called you to.

OVERCOMING DOUBT AND OPPOSITION

Sometimes, because of cultural and historical messages we've received about our place in God's mission and what we can't do as women, we hesitate and struggle to overcome doubt when His call comes. I (Cass) have wrestled with this for years.

I am probably the last person anyone would have thought would end up as a Bible teacher and author. Growing up, I had to fight hard for every passing grade I received. I failed most of my spelling tests and, if it weren't for the modern miracle of spell-check, I highly doubt I'd be writing this book today. On top of that, I ran with the wild crowd, the kind of kids who made mischief an art form. I was known for sneaking out at night, riding in cars with boys, and going to pasture parties (in the South, this is basically a bunch of juvenile delinquents drinking Boone's Farm wine coolers on someone's property in the middle of nowhere). I know, real classy. Thankfully, I was a teenager during the age of limited photographic evidence and, outside of MySpace, I didn't have a digital footprint or social media. Praise the Lord.

I dropped out of college when I got married, and once I became a wife and mother of three, I didn't consider going back to school a viable option. So I definitely didn't have any fancy credentials when I first started writing my blog to minister to other women. In fact, I often joke that I've got a one-dollar budget when people use pretentious five-dollar words in conversation with me. I didn't even grow up speaking the Christian lingo, and I would often find myself panicked when asked to turn to a particular book of the Bible during a Sunday sermon, as I wasn't sure I knew where to look for it.

With all this in mind, imagine my surprise when someone from the board of trustees at Denver Seminary reached out to me last summer and asked if I'd ever considered attending seminary. At first, I laughed it off. *She's got to be kidding, right? Me? There's no way!* I thought to myself. Then reality set in. She was serious. I've never felt more intimidated in my life. Earlier, I shared the story of my unlikely journey to becoming a seminarian, but what I didn't share was the intense opposition I faced after my decision to apply. It seemed that as soon as I decided to say yes to God, my physical health began to radically deteriorate without explanation, we had to sell what we thought was our dream house, and my mental health took a violent turn for the worse.

As if the physical and spiritual battle I was engulfed in wasn't enough for me to tuck tail and run, I also had people in my life I deeply respected telling me I was irresponsible for even considering applying as a woman, let alone attending in this season of life. Those critical comments cut me to the marrow of my soul and left me feeling deeply discouraged and inadequate. Self-doubt and fear became my constant companions. Nothing about my choice to pursue a master of biblical and theological studies degree made sense to me. How could God be calling me to do something so far outside of my intellectual and financial comfort zone? And why would He, if women weren't supposed to do this sort of thing in the first place?

IF THE ENEMY CAN SHUT DOWN AND SILENCE WOMEN, HE'S REMOVED HALF OF HIS OPPOSITION.

Here's a spiritual life hack for those of you in similar shoes: Expect resistance when waging war against the enemy of our souls. When God calls you to join Him in His work, the Enemy will do whatever he can to stop you, including making you doubt your calling. But consider this: There is more at stake than even your one contribution to the kingdom. What better way for the Enemy to defeat the church than to do it from within? More than half of evangelical protestant Christian church attendance is female. If the Enemy can shut down and silence women, he's removed half of his opposition. The powers and principalities of darkness don't take spiritual warfare lightly, and neither should we. Don't fear the pushback of the Enemy. Greater is He who is within you than He who is in the world (1 John 4:4), and Christ within you has already secured your victory.

Looking back now at the beginnings of my time in seminary, I recognize that total dependence on God is the sweet fruit produced through that sour season. I learned a lot about God during that first semester, but I also learned a lot about myself. I was forced to uproot the fear of inadequacy that had burrowed itself deep within me from a young age. I had to come to the end of myself to discover it's Christ alone who sustains me, not the approval of others or even my own strength.

I had to give up my desire to push past my limitations. I hit a wall, both literally and metaphorically. I could no longer muscle my way through the hard things, and I had to learn to accept that reality. There were days when just getting out of bed was a victory, as my body, mind, and spirit were so tired and weary. But I discovered the freedom found in total reliance upon the God of all capacity at work within me and through me. I found confidence in Christ's ability to increase my threshold for difficulty. Most importantly, I learned that God isn't deterred by our inadequacy or others' displeasure as we follow His leading. Rather, He sees our weakness and apparent disqualifications as an opportunity to point others to His all-surpassing sufficiency.

Life won't always make sense to me, and God's goodness won't always be clearly reflected in my reality, but Jesus is and will always be more than enough for me. Despite the obvious obstacles, God placed me exactly where He wanted me to be and opened doors that I'd never have had the audacity to knock on. I'm living proof that God can take someone who would otherwise be rendered useless and use them for His purpose.

DOING SCARY THINGS SCARED

Let's be honest, though. Embracing obedience when it's wrapped in fear is so hard. Sometimes, stepping into what God calls us to do feels a lot like being asked to dance on a stage—when you've never even learned the steps in detail.

This might surprise you, but speaking creates an intense physical manifestation of anxiety for me (Cass). I sweat profusely, my skin flushes bright red, my heart rate speeds up, my hands shake, and I struggle to catch my breath. This might be a little TMI, but I've even been known to experience panic attacks and toss my cookies the morning of a speaking engagement (gross, I know). This was such a regular occurrence that I developed a habit of eating an extremely light and bland breakfast before any event, just in case my nerves got the best of me. I used to say I have stage fright, but I no longer believe this to be true. This might seem woo-woo to some of you, but I've started to ask myself, *What does the Enemy stand to gain if I choose not to confront this discomfort?* And the answer is: a lot.

I'm beginning to view these physical obstacles as an indication of an unseen battle and an invitation to rely more deeply upon God instead of leaning on my own strength. Our adversary doesn't allow us to take back ground without a fight. Adversity is an indication that the Enemy isn't havin' it. In my case, this manifested physically, mentally, and spiritually. But I'm learning to embrace the nervousness that comes with walking in obedience. The sensation of anxiety that washes over me before I speak keeps me reverent and reliant on the Spirit.

I'm going to tell you something I wish someone had told me a long time ago: Doing it scared is sacred too. Our limitations keep us dependent on God. If you're walking through something that requires a great deal of faith, I see you and I believe in you. If you're taking one forward step even as others cluck disapprovingly at you, I see you and I believe in you. If you're even just dipping a toe into the waters of God's purpose for you while you battle the feelings of inadequacy that history, society, and culture have ingrained in you, I see you and I believe in you. More importantly, God sees you, and I believe in God's power at work within and through you. If that's you today, know that your lack of comfort in this season might not be an indication of a lack of God's provision but an invitation to trust.

I often think about this quote that we hear tossed around in Christian circles: "God would never give you anything that you can't handle." Every time I hear someone say that one-liner—a misquoted version of 1 Corinthians 10:13—I cringe a little bit, the reason being that sometimes we *are* given things we can't handle. Sometimes we *are* called to things we have no idea how to accomplish. The truth is that God *is* going to give us things we can't handle, because *He* can handle them. That's kind of the point I think we tend to miss. And it's the very reason we can do the scary things scared, because He ain't scared. He knows what He's doing. And, ultimately, He is with us. He gets the glory. He can handle what we cannot. We get to be obedient and partner with Him.

But here's the thing about obedience: It's rarely about feeling fully prepared or unquestionably confident. Obedience is stepping out even when your heart is racing and your hands are trembling. It's saying yes to God, even when your flesh screams for the comfort of familiarity, for the safety of coloring inside the lines.

Obedience, I've found, is often about doing the hard things scared. It's about trusting that God is weaving something beautiful out of our hesitant steps and faltering words. Sometimes courage only comes after obedience. God can accomplish extraordinary things with our ordinary acts of courageous obedience.

Remember, God isn't looking at our qualifications; He's looking for our willingness. He's seeking a heart that says, "Here I am, Lord, use me, even if I'm afraid or unsure."

And what does He do? He uses that *willingness* more than our *skill*, our *trust* more than our *talent*, and our *obedience* more than our *ability*.

As we close this chapter, let's reflect on the journey we've embarked upon together. We've delved into the depths of uncertainty, wrestled with self-doubt, and faced opposition head-on. Yet, through it all, one truth has remained steadfast: Our calling as women of God transcends societal norms and theological debates. It emanates from the very heart of God, beckoning us to step into the sacred space of living on mission. In the cacophony of voices clamoring for our attention, let us tune our ears to the gentle whisper of our Creator, who calls us by name and equips us for every task He has set before us. Our place and purpose within the body of Christ aren't contingent on the approval of others or the confines of tradition. Instead, our qualification is firmly rooted in the God who has created and commissioned us.

As you navigate the uncharted waters of your calling, remember this: You're not alone. The same God who walked alongside Deborah on the battlefield, who empowered Mary Magdalene to proclaim the good news, and who emboldened Phoebe to carry Paul's letter to Rome is with you today. His presence is your strength, His wisdom is your guide, and

His love is your light guiding you onward in your God-given purpose.

So, will you say yes? Will you step boldly onto the path God has placed before you, knowing that He who calls you is faithful to fulfill His purpose in and through you? Will you choose to embrace God's all-surpassing sufficiency in the face of inadequacy? The journey may be daunting, the pavement might be rough, and the path might be uncertain, but through it all, this remains true: You can do this, because God is with you.

Yes, you, with all your fears, insecurities, and hesitations. You are wildly capable, not because of your own merit, but because of the One who walks before, behind, and alongside you. The mighty power of the God of the universe, the Creator of the heavens and earth, is with you.

So, what do you say? Are you ready to live a life on mission for God? For the glory of His name and the advancement of His kingdom, let's give God our yes. When we choose to believe in His power at work within and through us, we discover the truest and most fulfilling expression of our purpose: to know Him, be known by Him, and to make Him known, for now and all eternity.

It's time to stop pursuing permission and start living on mission.

REFLECTION QUESTIONS

1. Have you ever hesitated to pursue a calling due to fear of overstepping perceived scriptural or societal boundaries?

2. In what ways have you experienced the tension between seeking God's approval and the approval of others regarding your role in the church or community?

3. Reflect on a time when you were called to step out in faith despite feeling inadequate. How did this experience shape your understanding of God's sufficiency?

4. What does "doing scary things scared" look like in your own life? Share a personal experience when you moved forward in obedience despite fear or hesitation.

SIX

ANSWERING HIS CALL

I (Britt) can still recall the unmistakable aroma of books and freshly brewed coffee as we perused our local Barnes & Noble. The hushed sounds of footsteps and muted phone rings filled the background. I, a new Christian, wandered the aisles, taking in the extensive collection of Christian literature. A soft snicker drew me to my group of friends from college ministry right around the corner, their attention fixed on a book they deemed lacking in theological depth. To my astonishment, one even hid this particular book on the shelf behind the others that were more "appropriately written," in their estimation.

I couldn't help but wonder about the emotional weight of having one's words so critically judged. I know now that as an author you feel an immense responsibility knowing your written words might be the very thing someone needs to push them toward a leap of faith. I felt a pang of sympathy—how heartbreaking to have one's heart and soul poured into those pages and then dismissed so casually! It was then and is still disheartening. I recall thinking, *I could never bear to face such scrutiny or rejection.* Yet, here I am, typing on my laptop, writing my third book, and penning my thoughts on purpose. God is funny that way, isn't He? I could never have envisioned this particular chapter of my life, yet every small act of obedience in the micro moments, every whispered prayer, every trial, led me right here, to this moment.

Yet, even before the idea of authoring books ever took root in my heart, that incident at Barnes & Noble planted seeds of doubt and fear. You might wonder how such a minor event could overshadow the path God eventually called me to walk, but you have to understand that my life has always been shadowed by fear—be it the fear of the unknown, fear of rejection, or the fear of failure. Reflecting on that day, I've discerned the Enemy's ploy through the actions of my friends, trying to cause me to dismiss a calling before God even whispered it into my heart. I unknowingly took myself out of the game before I was called to pick up my bat. Has this ever happened to you?

That brings me to my first question for you: What is God whispering into your heart right now? Could it possibly be something you, like myself, have unknowingly dismissed years ago? How has the Enemy caused you to doubt what God might be leading you to?

Perhaps you've felt a subtle nudge or a quiet pull, maybe even toward something miles outside of your comfort zone.

Maybe there's a memory from years past that keeps surfacing unexpectedly. Or a dream planted by God in your heart awaiting the right moment, the right conditions to sprout and flourish. If so, it's definitely worth exploring through prayer, friend. It could be God gently reminding you of a calling, a purpose, or a passion you once felt but wrote off.

Just like my memory of that Barnes & Noble incident, you might have experienced moments when something seemingly insignificant steered you away from a path God intended for you. Moments when fear, apprehension, or even the opinions of others caused you to dismiss yourself. The good news? As long as we have a pulse, God's plans for us don't expire, even if we take a wrong turn out of fear. They remain, sometimes dormant, waiting for us to rediscover them through the power of the Holy Spirit.

GOD'S PLANS FOR US DON'T EXPIRE, EVEN IF WE TAKE A WRONG TURN OUT OF FEAR.

My next question for you to consider is this: What might you uncover if you dared to listen to those whispers from God once again?

I've learned that if we are inactive and unresponsive to God's whispers, it doesn't mean they diminish. They merely wait, just as an ember waits under the ash for a gust of wind to reignite its fire. Our callings, even when buried deep in the recesses of our fears and doubts, await the right moment to glow brightly. It's about rekindling that deep connection with our Creator and allowing Him to lead our steps. So, as you dive deeper into this chapter, ask yourself, *Have there been moments in my life when a calling felt so distant, so outside the realm of possibility, that I silenced its whisper? Moments when I opted for comfort over purpose?*

As you journey with us through our own revelations and struggles, we hope you rediscover those hidden whispers, those shelved macro dreams, and recognize that God's calls never fade; they simply await our yes.

THE SPARK OF HIS CALLING

Our lives often don't follow a linear trajectory. Just when we think we have it all figured out and mapped out, an unexpected nudge from the Lord can set us on a course we never envisioned for ourselves. For me (Britt), this unexpected nudge was to write.

Just four short years ago, God's call to me was unmistakably clear: to write books in this season of my life. To many, that might seem like a straightforward journey, one that most would be thrilled about. But if you truly knew me, you'd grasp the profound leap and immense discomfort it represented. You see, I've always thrived behind the scenes, content helping others accomplish a greater macro purpose, dedicated to serving without the need for recognition. As Her True Worth began to grow tremendously, I recognized a pressing need to channel the message of worth in Christ and purpose into something tangible for our community.

It was never my intention to establish this ministry as a launchpad for authorship or to seek renown. My heart has been set on a singular mission: to share Jesus and the gospel in a space where self-centric narratives often dominate: social media.

After countless hours of prayer, reflection, and soul-searching conversations with Cass and the Lord, it became clear that writing was the next step for this ministry. It offered a deeper, more intimate avenue to touch the hearts and lives of our community.

Now enter into my discomfort.

I joke with my husband that I see so much of Moses in myself. Moses, the reluctant leader, the one who felt so inadequate and ill-equipped for the mission God set before him. When God called Moses to lead the Israelites out of Egypt, his immediate reaction was one of doubt. "Who am I that I should go to Pharaoh and bring the Israelites out of Egypt?" he asked (Exodus 3:11 NIV).

Wow. That is a sentiment I know all too well. Maybe you do too. It's still echoing in my heart as I contemplate the magnitude of pouring out my thoughts for the world to read. Moses' uncertainty resonates deeply within me. Perhaps you've felt that same tug of doubt, the same whisper of hesitancy? I often grapple with similar thoughts, such as, *Who am I, that others would want to read these words?* and *Who am I, Lord, that You'd entrust me with such a task and responsibility?* It's a recurring refrain: "Who am I . . . ?"

Amid these whirlwind emotions and questions, a grounding and freeing truth emerges every single time—it's not about me; it's about Him. This realization isn't just a fleeting thought but a profound understanding that anchors my very existence.

I've missed the whole point if I think I'm doing all this for myself or to find out who I am through what I do. We live in a world where individual achievements, personal successes, and self-promotion often take center stage. And while there's nothing wrong with celebrating personal milestones, we must never forget the source of our strength and our abilities.

Remember Jesus' words: "I am the vine; you are the branches. Whoever abides in me and I in him, he it is that bears much fruit, for apart from me you can do nothing" (John 15:5). This metaphor is both beautiful and instructive. As branches, our purpose and vitality are linked to the vine. When we bear fruit, it is not for our glory but for the glorification of the vine, from which we draw life. When we succeed, it's a testament to His grace, His provision, and His power working through us. When we face challenges, it's an invitation to lean even more into His embrace, trusting that the Master Vinedresser knows exactly when to prune, when to water, and when to harvest. We need only sow and give our yes.

Even if all you have is the humble offering of a single penny, when given with a willing heart, it becomes enough in His hands. Just like Jesus' mustard-seed analogy: A miniscule seed grows into a massive tree with time and nurturing. It doesn't take monumental faith—just a mustard seed of it—to step into what He is calling us to do, trusting that He will walk with us.

Let's go back to Moses. The beauty of his story, and indeed mine, lies not in immediate readiness but in a journey of trust. Moses had his reservations, his insecurities, and his perceived limitations. I did too. And *still* do. However, God isn't seeking a perfect leader, a perfect author, or a perfect anything, just a willing heart. Moses, despite his hesitations and insecurities, was willing to be molded, to learn, and to trust. Are we? Do we dare to trust Him with our yes, even if we think we have little to offer?

Awareness of our shortcomings can so often lead to insecurities. And insecurities can either be poison to our purpose or things that propel us into the Father's arms. Friend, it's this middle ground, the space between our willingness and our perceived limitations, where God often does His most beautiful work. When we lay bare our insecurities and doubts, He meets us there, reminding us that it's not by our strength but by His that we can achieve the purpose He has set for us in each season.

Just as Moses had Aaron and the support of God's signs and wonders, we, too, are never alone in our callings. I had Cass, and Cass had me. Together, God beautifully crafted a message from both our hearts to encourage the lives of others through the written word.

Rest in this: He knows. He knows what you need before you even figure out the words to ask. God supplies those whom He calls with what they'll need along the way. He turns perceived weaknesses into strengths and doubts into opportunities to activate an unwavering faith. Our role, much like Moses', is not to be instantly able but to be eternally willing. In that willingness, that surrender, lies the beauty of complete and total reliance upon the hands that carry us.

Maybe right now you don't feel able or capable. And that's okay. In fact, that's a good place to be, knowing that your Father can supply you with all the strength you could ever need. It's often said that God doesn't call the equipped; He equips the called. And He calls all of us, including you. This holds true for every journey we embark upon with Him, every challenge we take on in His name. While it's natural to doubt our worthiness or readiness, remember that it's not about our ability but our availability to God's will.

Are you willing?

COURAGE COMES AFTER OBEDIENCE

Once we say yes to God's call, one that feels bigger than we know how to pursue, there's an electrifying moment as we stand on the borders of upcoming change. Just a heartbeat away from stepping into something new and unknown. It's a mixture of fear, excitement, and anticipation. We often call this the "leap of faith." But what does that leap truly entail?

The apostle Peter had just such a defining moment of faith when he stepped out of the boat to walk on water toward Jesus (Matthew 14:29). Can you imagine what he felt in that moment? Completely unsure if he would succeed but completely sure His Lord had him every step of the way. And, by the way, this wasn't a casual stroll; it was a bold step filled with trust, fraught with doubt, and defying all human logic.

In that fleeting moment, Peter exemplified what it means to take a leap of faith, to move forward even when the odds, and perhaps even our own understanding, are against us. That's the essence of the leap. It's an action based not on what we see or feel, but on whom we trust.

Notice the two-part theme here. Trusting and taking action are dance partners when it comes to fulfilling our God-given purpose. One leads, and the other follows. But both are essential to the completion of the dance.

Trust lies at the very core of our faith. It's the bedrock upon which our relationship with God is built. Without trust, faith wanes and our foundation can become shaky. Imagine trust as the anchor that steadies a ship amid tumultuous waves; it grounds us and keeps us from being swayed by the winds. Trust isn't passive; it's a conscious choice.

TRUST ISN'T PASSIVE; IT'S A CONSCIOUS CHOICE.

Trust alone, though, without actions, can leave us stagnant. Faith, true faith, is active. It's a dynamic interplay of belief and deed. When James said, "Faith apart from works is useless" (James 2:20), he emphasized that our trust in God propels us into purposeful action. Think of Moses at the Red Sea. Yes, he trusted God, but he also had to act and stretch out his staff over the waters. Esther trusted God, but she also approached the king, risking her life for her people. Trust set the stage, but action played out the scene.

Often, when we think of taking a leap of faith, our minds come up with images of audacious jumps into the unknown, a blind plunge into uncharted territories. But what if we told you that most of our spiritual leaps, our demonstrations of bold trust in action, are actually the culmination of countless smaller, intentional moments of growth, trust, and surrender? What if, all along, the Lord has been preparing us?

Peter's step out of the boat and onto the turbulent waters on the surface appeared to be a massive leap of faith. But let's not forget the fact that Peter literally walked with the Savior of the world. The experiences, lessons, and moments he encountered with Jesus all led up to that defining event. He'd witnessed Jesus turning water into wine, feeding thousands with a meager offering, and healing the sick and afflicted. Peter had shared meals with Him, engaged in deep conversations, and marveled at the profound wisdom Jesus imparted. Each of these moments was a thread that strengthened Peter's bond of trust with Jesus, fostering an understanding that Christ was who He said He was.

It wasn't a subtle impulse that propelled Peter out of the boat; it was a reservoir of experiences with Jesus that rendered him hopelessly lost without Jesus. This leap was just the outward manifestation of the trust he'd been building over time—or, rather, the trust Jesus had been building in him.

Think of it like a dam. Over time, water (or, in this case, trust) builds up behind the dam, accumulating with every experience and every testimony. And then, at the opportune moment, the dam's gates are opened and the water rushes forward. That's Peter stepping out of the boat. The trust had been building, and this was its powerful release.

The misconception we often carry is that faith is about one giant leap.

Instead, faith is cultivated in the everyday moments, in the quiet times of prayer, in the times of waiting, worship, and in the moments of surrender.

It's in these moments that we're primed and prepared for the times we're called to step out in boldness.

Peter's step onto the water wasn't his first act of faith. It was a significant one, but it was built on a foundation of countless moments of trust and surrender. And perhaps the most beautiful aspect of this is that Jesus was there for every single one of those moments, teaching, guiding, and preparing Peter, along with the other disciples.

In reflecting on Peter's story and my (Britt's) own, it's clear that every small act of obedience and every moment of trust plays a significant role in answering God's call. From the quiet reflections in a bookstore to the decisive steps toward writing, these experiences illustrate how our callings unfold through life's simple interactions and the Spirit's quiet nudges. Each act of overcoming fear and stepping into faith is a crucial building block in God's larger plan.

As we move into the theme of resilience, it's essential to recognize that our spiritual endurance and ability to rise above challenges are constructed from these small, yet powerful, moments. Embrace this incremental journey of faith and trust, knowing that God is actively shaping you for the challenges and triumphs that lie ahead.

REFLECTION QUESTIONS

1. How have you navigated through moments when criticism or judgment made you question your calling?

2. Can you think of a dream you shelved because of fear or doubt? How might revisiting it now serve God's purpose for you?

3. Describe a time when a small act of obedience became a significant turning point in your faith journey.

4. Think about a time when you realized your accomplishments were less about your own capabilities and more about God working through you. How does this change the way you view your successes and failures?

SEVEN

THE SHAPE OF RESILIENCE

Have you ever seen a tree grow into its surroundings? There's a place called the Crooked Forest in Poland where the pine trees haven't grown straight up toward the sky like most trees do, but instead each one has a weird twist. Literally. They all curve at the base, then go straight back up. It's like each tree decided to take a turn right at the start of its life before heading upward!

Life can sometimes push us in unexpected directions, much like the weirdly shaped trees. We might start off thinking we've got a clear directive or a straight shot at where we're going, but then *bam!* Life happens. We're talking about those personal ups and downs, unexpected changes, or even those moments when something just clicks spiritually and you feel the need to take a leap in a new direction. Here's the cool part: These twists and turns aren't us going off track. They're part of how we grow.

This journey of purpose isn't linear; it's a beautiful, complex path that intertwines our daily actions with God's overarching plan for our lives. Our purpose shifts and morphs as we grow, molded by the sovereign hands that shape us. Through all our seasons, trials, and transformations, it's truly God's constancy that anchors us.

When I (Cass) first started my journey toward becoming an author and ministry leader, I was sitting inside Saint Michael's Neonatal Intensive Care Unit in Texarkana, Texas. Our youngest son, Everett, had been born eight weeks premature in an emergency C-section, due to my having preeclampsia. We both nearly lost our lives. It was a grueling experience—having my baby taken away, lying alone in my hospital bed for more than twenty-four hours, being treated with magnesium sulfate (in order to prevent seizures or stroke due to pregnancy-induced high blood pressure). All I could do was cry and pray.

The first time I held our son he was attached to a tangle of tubes and medical equipment. His fragile body weighed under three pounds. As the NICU nurse placed him on my chest, I remember her telling us that our son couldn't suck, swallow, or breathe without machines. I wept uncontrollably. It was one of the scariest moments of my life. My heart was flooded with anxiety and uncertainty. But amid this turmoil, a new path was being carved for me.

My husband had accepted a job in Oklahoma City at Tinker Air Force Base, and he had to report back to work twenty-four hours after our son was delivered. In my attempt to sort out what I was walking through, I decided to write about it. I processed my grief with raw honesty, a little bit of humor, and a whole lot of Jesus. There I was, a mother of three children, ages three and under, with a house to sell and no idea what the future had in store for me.

Until this point, I was a hair-and-makeup artist. I had no ministry or writing credentials or resources, but still I decided to write. I admit, at first I was writing for myself. It was cathartic, and I've always processed my emotions through journaling. I never intended to do it publicly. Then one day I somehow had the courage to post my experience online, and someone reached out to me. It was a woman who had experienced the same thing, saying how much my post had meant to her and that she felt seen. Not to be dramatic, but that moment changed the trajectory of my life.

I can't help but marvel at how God weaves our personal trials and victories into His greater purpose.

Did my writing go viral? No. And no big publishers were looking at me, but in that moment, I felt a spark of certainty that I hadn't felt before. I knew I was supposed to use my words to point weary, wounded, and wandering women to the hope we have in Jesus.

In my despair, God used our son's turbulent delivery to awaken a passion I didn't even realize was lying dormant inside of me. So what did I do next? I purchased a WordPress website domain on credit, because we didn't have the money, and I called my blog *Speer and Arrows*, because it was catchy.

We were in the middle of a major life transition, changing careers, selling our home in Texas, hospital bills piling up, house hunting in Oklahoma, trying to raise our girls, and bonding with our son through a glass box. All while my husband worked hours away in a different state. It didn't make sense that I'd stop doing what I had always done to pursue something I had no idea how to do. And yet, I did. I was listening to podcasts while pumping breast milk for our son, reading blogs on Pinterest, and teaching myself how to build a website (it wasn't great). I didn't know what God was up to, but looking back I can see His sovereignty with clarity. His goodness was woven throughout every detail of that period of our lives.

I had no promise of success, little money, and hardly any sleep, but in that moment, I knew that I was right where I was supposed to be. If only one person read what I wrote and was led to hope, I would know I had accomplished what I set out to do. If no one saw it, I would know I was obedient to God, who was worthy of everything I had to give. I didn't need to have all the resources, the qualifications, or the prestigious education in order to obey God. I was responsible for showing up where I was with what I had, and God was responsible for the results.

We won't always see or understand the impact of our choice

to trust and obey God on this side of heaven, but I can promise you this: Each small step of obedience is woven into God's mission for humanity, even in the face of adversity. The small adds up to the grand.

My transition from a hair-and-makeup artist to a voice of hope and comfort through my writing is a prime example of the dynamic nature of purpose. The unexpected turn of events that led to the birth of my son was not just a challenging phase; it marked the beginning of a new path, a new way God intended to use my life for His glory.

I am often encouraged by this verse, and I hope you will be, too, as you continue on this journey: "We are afflicted in every way, but not crushed; perplexed, but not driven to despair; persecuted, but not forsaken; struck down, but not destroyed" (2 Corinthians 4:8–9).

WHEN THE ROAD IS ROUGH

I'm going to tell you something I wish someone had told me (Cass) fifteen years ago. Living a life for Christ and pursuing our purpose doesn't exempt us from facing hardships. Despite our best efforts and intentions, challenges are an integral part of the journey. I'm slightly embarrassed to admit that when I was still young in my faith, I wrestled with the concept that life would still be hard even after I chose to follow Jesus. I had this preconceived notion that dedicating my life to God and asking

Jesus into my heart would come with the abundant life promised in John 10:10. Bless my naïve little heart.

I had no idea that, although Jesus had conquered the gates
of hell to win my soul, I'd still encounter heartache and hardships on this side of heaven. I'm not sure if my misconception
was something directly taught to me or if I came up with this
based upon my own lack of understanding, but I arrived at the
conclusion that being a Christian would somehow make my
life better. So I checked all the imaginary boxes that I thought
would please God. I attended church every time the doors were
open, and I volunteered my free time and participated on the
prayer team. You can imagine my disappointment when life
continued to be *life*, and my circumstances didn't magically
improve.

I'll never forget the Thursday night church service I
attended when I bravely went up for prayer during the altar call.
I felt convicted that I wasn't honoring God with my finances
and admitted I was struggling to trust God's provision in my
life. A slightly older girl placed her hands on my shoulders, and
we prayed together. I remember walking away feeling lighter
and relieved to leave my burdens at the altar. Little did I know,
I was about to lose my dream job the following week, which
would devastate me.

I had recently gone through a difficult breakup and now
was unemployed. Things were looking grim. I felt like I had
been bamboozled by God. When I returned to church the following week, I sulked in the back row. *This? This is what I get*

when I place my trust in You? I quietly scoffed as I held back tears. I know how ridiculous I sound admitting that to you right now, but twenty-one-year-old Cass was straight up not having a good time. I was confused and struggling to reconcile how God could be good while the reality of my situation was not. Where was that abundant life I was promised? Why couldn't I just pray all my problems away? I thought no weapons formed against me could prosper (Isaiah 54:17), but it looked to me like these weapons were prosperin'. I wish I could tell you that I outgrew that mentality but, unfortunately, I'm a slow learner.

My husband and I recently celebrated our tenth wedding anniversary. That tenth year was such a milestone, but it was also the hardest year of our marriage yet. We had made the decision to build what we thought would be our dream home, but that dream would become our worst nightmare. We got in over our heads and couldn't keep up with the financial demands of our lives. The cost of everything increased in a matter of months while our income remained the same. We were house poor and didn't know how to escape this mistake we had made.

The day I found out we were behind on our mortgage was a sobering one. I felt like a failure, like it was all my fault. I was the one who wanted the shiny, new, aesthetically pleasing house. I was the one who wanted the fourth bedroom and the home office that we didn't need. Now here we were, drowning in debt, in over our heads. It was clear that we needed to sell our home and downsize, but the housing market was at a standstill. Nothing was selling. We went from houses rapidly selling to our home sitting on the market from April to August without any interest from buyers. To say it was excruciating would be an understatement.

We received varying responses from the people closest to us as we shared our struggle. We were offered support, but we also sensed harsh judgment. It was gut-wrenching. I found myself feeling forgotten by God yet again. We were in a deep hole, and I was the one holding the shovel.

There's a scripture I've learned to cling to when it feels like everything is going wrong:

> Consider it a great joy, my brothers and sisters, whenever you experience various trials, because you know that the testing of your faith produces endurance. And let endurance have its full effect, so that you may be mature and complete, lacking nothing. (James 1:2–4 CSB)

Notice that James tells us to consider it joy *when* we experience various trials, not *if*. He's urging his reader to be proactive in their response to trials instead of being reactive, because the truth is, crisis comes for us all. Our health might fail us, a marriage might end, we might lose a loved one, or we might face financial failures, trauma, addictions, and disappointments. The list could go on and on, but I think you get the point. Although we will suffer various difficulties in this life, we should consider it joy. Why? Because the testing of our faith produces endurance.

Let's pause here for a moment and ponder that sentence. I want to squirm in my chair when I consider the juxtaposition of joy with trials. These two words seem to be opposites, yet James is implying they belong hand in hand. You might be uncomfortable with this concept. If you are, you're in good company. But let's look a bit closer at the text.

James told us our trials produce endurance through the testing of our faith. I think it's important to recognize that encountering hardships is not a sign of failure or lack of faith, but rather an essential aspect of spiritual growth. I imagine endurance being built like a muscle in response to adversity. The more you encounter this rough terrain, the more your faith muscle builds a tolerance for resistance. That's good news! You see, the more we walk through difficulty, the more our faith endures. The more endurance we acquire, the more spiritual maturity we develop. In other words, we can shift our perspective in the midst of adversity, because we're able to recognize that even what the Enemy intends for evil God is able to use for the ultimate good (Genesis 50:20). And that, my friend, is something that brings me great joy!

I know it might be hard to see it now, but God is able to create beauty from our heartache. The difficulties we encounter test and refine our commitment to our calling. They reveal our true strengths and weaknesses, allowing us to grow and develop a more sincere faith. Navigating difficulties today helps us stay grounded in our purpose, reminding us of the importance of perseverance and determination tomorrow. The multitude of trials we experience, when viewed together, create a beautiful mosaic that our eyes cannot yet comprehend. There is so much happening in the unseen realms of our lives, but the abundance of God isn't reliant upon our health, wealth, or popularity. We're human, we make mistakes, and life doesn't always go our way, but God's sovereignty remains unchanged.

As I grow in my walk with God, I'm learning that His goodness doesn't negate the heartache we experience. In fact, His mercy is that much sweeter once we've tasted the bitterness of this life. I used to believe that pursuing my calling would result in a perfect, trouble-free journey. I've heard experience is an effective teacher, and I believe this to be true. Now that I've lived a bit more life, I've experienced my fair share of bumps and bruises, and I'm beginning to view pain as a trustworthy teacher.

I'm not going to pretend I'm an expert at this. I'm learning this lesson alongside you. But let's remember this: with God's guidance, we can be transformed by the imperfect circumstances we encounter instead of being taken out by them. Each perceived loss is a learning opportunity rather than a hindrance to our calling. Let's choose to lean into our hardships, knowing that each trial strengthens our spiritual muscle and equips us to press onward toward our purpose, even when the road is rough.

God is faithful to walk alongside us as we learn the hard lessons of life, even if that means we learn the same lesson a few times.

I like to think God is like the artist Bob Ross. Carefully creating with every brushstroke, He repurposes our messes into a beautiful canvas, displaying His loving-kindness. So each time you are faced with what seem to be shortcomings, let them be a reminder that it's an opportunity for the Lord's strength to shine through those broken cracks.

WITH GOD'S GUIDANCE, WE CAN BE TRANSFORMED BY THE IMPERFECT CIRCUMSTANCES WE ENCOUNTER INSTEAD OF BEING TAKEN OUT BY THEM.

OVERCOMING SPIRITUAL SETBACKS

We've established that adversity is a crucial part of our faith journey. Without resistance, we would never build stamina or endurance. It's true that some storms come to destroy us and take us off the map, but other storms come to water what God is growing within us and redirect our path. It's the overcoming that builds our endurance and helps us develop a sincere faith that has emerged from the refining fires of life. C. S. Lewis wrote, "We can ignore even pleasure. But pain insists upon being attended to. God whispers to us in our pleasures, speaks in our conscience, but shouts in our pains: it is his megaphone to rouse a deaf world."[1] In other words, suffering wakes us up. Perhaps it's time we view pain as a tool to be used for God's purpose instead of an enemy against it.

As someone who has done extensive prolonged exposure therapy to overcome complex childhood trauma and abuse, the last sentence makes me wince as I write it. The idea that there is purpose in our pain, that the things God can grow out of it make it worth it, has never settled well with me. But that doesn't make it untrue. My friend Toni Collier recently said on a podcast that "pain isn't ever worth it, but God never wastes it."[2] The truth is, it might not ever feel like the heartache we endured was worth it. Still, that doesn't mean God will waste it. Both of these things can be true at the same time.

I want to be clear, especially to those of us who've endured pain at the hands of those who should've been safe, that this isn't my attempt to minimize or excuse what happened to you. What I am saying is, even our pain can be used for the glory of God and the good of others if we allow it. Pain may slow down our pace, but it doesn't have to dictate our destination.

Instead of allowing our pain to define us, we can choose to let it refine us. Pain doesn't have to derail us from following God's purpose for our lives. Rather, it's an opportunity for growth, resilience, and transformation. If we let God do His redeeming work in the middle of it, it can become a catalyst for deeper empathy and greater compassion, and it can help us to develop a more sincere faith.

PAIN MAY SLOW DOWN OUR PACE, BUT IT DOESN'T HAVE TO DICTATE OUR DESTINATION.

But there will come a moment in each of our lives that shakes our faith and might even leave a few cracks in our foundation. These are the moments when we wrestle with the reality of the cruelty of life on this side of heaven. Yes, it's precisely in these moments of trials and tears that our commitment to our calling is put to the test. This moment for me was in March 2022. I received a startling call that brought me to my knees.

My mother informed me that my Grandma Jan had been diagnosed with terminal cancer. She urged me to come quickly, because she was living on borrowed time. As mentioned in a previous chapter, this woman was "my person"; she practically raised me. I was in the midst of the final edits of our first book, *Her True Worth*, when I flew from Oklahoma to Wisconsin to be at her bedside. When I first arrived at the hospital, she was her usual feisty self, making sarcastic comments to the nurses and cussing out my relatives. Grandma Jan was always sweet, but she was never soft. Life didn't allow her the luxury of fragility. She was sharp and always spoke her mind, but as the days progressed, so did her rapid physical and cognitive deterioration.

The cancer was aggressive and spreading. The doctor informed us hospice wasn't going to be an option and that our primary goal was to make her as comfortable as possible before her passing. At that moment, it felt like all the air had been sucked out of that sterile hospital room. It felt like none of us could breathe. And as we listened to the doctor's words, I began to disassociate.

Looking back on that week I spent by Grandma Jan's side, I have a lot of regrets. I carried my work bag with me every day and would open my laptop to answer emails and work on the book. Some might say I was just being responsible, maybe even being faithful to my calling and mission, but the truth was I was running from the pain I needed to fully feel and process in order to heal. I wish I had allowed myself to stay fully present in it instead of trying to busily work it away. I wanted to escape reality so badly.

I checked out emotionally when I overheard my aunts and uncle bickering. Everyone was beyond their threshold of tolerance, and I was struggling to keep my composure. I snapped back into my childhood coping mechanisms for when things got overwhelming. When everyone else was sobbing, I held in my inner turmoil until I could make it back to my hotel room that evening. Someone had to hold it together for her; it might as well be me. She was always there for me, after all.

For the first time in my life, I remember questioning God, "How could You allow this to happen to her?" It seemed that all this woman had known was a life of sorrow. My Grandma Jan was a first-generation American. Her parents were immigrants, and her childhood wasn't easy. Her first marriage was to an abusive man who nearly killed her, and her second was to my paternal grandfather, a veteran with severe PTSD.

After her second marriage came to an end, she endured homelessness as a single mother of four and temporarily lost custody to the foster-care system that seemed to treat her poverty as a punishable offense. There was so much heartache in her life, yet hers was the biggest heart I'd ever known. She cared for people fervently and never judged a book by its cover. She offered mercy freely, and what little she had she was always willing to share.

I remember one of the final days we spent together before she lost her ability to speak. She was talking to me about myself as a baby, almost as if I wasn't in the room or she no longer recognized me. I'm grateful I had the forethought to get a recording of what she was saying to me, although two years later, I still haven't been able to bring myself to listen to it. I was leaning on her bed, holding her hand, as her eyes began to drift up toward the ceiling. She stopped speaking and began to stare intently. I sat there in silence with her for a few minutes before my curiosity got the best of me.

"What are we looking at?" I asked.

"Where I think I'm going," she replied.

"Where you *think* you're going?" I repeated back to her.

"Yes, well . . . where I hope I'm going," she said sheepishly.

"You *hope*?!" I replied, as we both burst out into laughter. I can still hear her boisterous laugh. If only I could go back to that moment and ask more questions! What did she see above her on the ceiling? Did she see Jesus, a bright light, or golden streets? One day, I'll get to ask her when I meet her on the other side of eternity, but for now I'm left with my curiosity.

The loss of my grandmother is still something that aches within my soul. The first year of grief felt like a spiritual setback for me. It left me disappointed with God and questioning everything. Why would a God of love allow Grandma Jan to lead such a painful life, followed by such a painful ending? How could I trust Him with my own future? With the path that I'd thought I should be walking? Was it always going to be this hard? Was there a point in me continuing to follow His leading?

Some scholars call what I was experiencing "the dark night of the soul." The phrase comes from a poem written by Saint John of the Cross, a sixteenth-century poet and mystic. In it, he describes the journey of a soul and the unknowable nature of God as "a dark night." I found a strange sense of comfort upon my discovery that the spiritual depression and regression I was treading through wasn't an experience unique to me but rather a phenomenon that's been endured by many believers before me and alongside me.

John Mark Comer described his dark night like this: "God is graciously allowing me to experience my own emptiness apart from him."[3] As much as it pains me to admit, this resonates with me. At first, I felt like God had removed Himself from me in my grief, but now I recognize it wasn't His presence but the things I attached to His goodness that were taken from me. Eventually that loss freed me to see God more clearly. The darkness of the soul won't last forever, but within it is a precious truth that will endure the test of time: In the darkness, His light shines brighter (John 1:5).

As I saw during my dark night, heartache and hardship in its various forms can significantly impact our ability to pursue our calling and walk out our mission faithfully. It does this in four ways.

- **Distraction and Disruption.** Pain can distract us from our purpose and disrupt our focus. Whether it's physical, emotional, relational, or spiritual pain, it can consume our thoughts and energy, making it hard to stay committed to our calling.
- **Fear and Resistance.** Pain can trigger fear and resistance. Especially if it's associated with past failures or traumas. We might fear repeating past mistakes or reliving the worst moments of our lives, which can lead to avoidance and hesitation when pursuing our calling.
- **Doubt and Discouragement.** Pain can lead to doubt and discouragement, causing us to call into question our identity, spiritual gifts, abilities, and the validity of our calling. It may shake our confidence and create despair, hindering our progress toward pursuing our purpose.
- **Emotional Exhaustion.** Dealing with pain can drain us emotionally, leaving us feeling depressed and depleted. There's a reason Proverbs 13:12 tells us, "Hope deferred makes the heart sick." This weariness of the soul can make it challenging to muster the energy and gumption needed to pursue our calling with passion, hope, and sincere enthusiasm.

The good news is, we don't have to feel stuck here. Whether you're facing your dark night of the soul or are simply struggling through a painful season, you can persevere through that pain and continue living on mission faithfully. Here are four ways I've learned to do just that.

- **Seek Healing.** We can't heal what we aren't willing to feel. Addressing the source of our pain through therapy or godly counsel can help lessen the impact it has on our lives. Pursuing healing helps us process and release the pain we're experiencing, empowering us to move forward.
- **Cultivate Resilience.** Building resilience equips us to navigate challenges and setbacks without losing sight of our calling. By developing resilience, we learn to bounce back from pain stronger and more determined than before, allowing us to persevere in the face of adversity.
- **Fortify Faith.** Trusting and leaning on God through adversity fortifies our faith by creating endurance and developing character, allowing us to persevere in the face of adversity.
- **Receive Compassion.** Showing ourselves kindness and receiving the compassion of others in moments of pain fosters self-acceptance and resilience. Treating ourselves with gentleness and understanding allows us to acknowledge our pain without letting it stifle us, empowering us to continue pursuing our calling with grace and perseverance.

As we encounter the valleys of adversity, it's natural to question the purpose behind our pain and the seeming silence of the

Divine. It's common to wonder if we've gotten things wrong or if we should stay on the path. In our questions and frustrations, let us hold fast to the assurance that God's purpose is at work, even when we cannot see it. And may we find comfort in the truth that, though the night may be long, the dawn always breaks, illuminating the path forward with newfound clarity and strength. May our hearts be filled with hope, our steps guided by faith, and our souls anchored in the unwavering love of our Creator.

DILIGENCE IN THE DARK

You know what's comforting to think about, considering the way so many of us eventually walk through a dark night of the soul? God tends to do some of His best work in the dark. Just as there is a purpose for sunlight to grow and sustain life, God intentionally created the night. Some things can only be brought to life in the dark and the unseen moments. Think of seeds when they're planted deep beneath the earth's surface, or a baby forming in its mother's womb, or even a photograph that needs to be developed in a room devoid of light.

I (Cass) was recently at a backyard birthday party where the backyard was like a wild and majestic garden, filled with all kinds of plants and crawling creatures. I'm fairly certain the family hosting the party were homesteaders, raising their own animals and growing their own vegetables to eat. I stumbled up to a plant that resembled a large white pepper from a distance, but the closer I got, the more I began to wonder what it was. It was a closed moonflower, a plant that blooms only after the sun has set. It releases a beautiful aroma into the evening air and has a spiky sharp circular seed pod that hardens and eventually falls off the plant to begin its life cycle again. Eventually, that unattractive and possibly dangerous pod will find itself beneath the surface, bursting forth through the soil to become a new moonflower.

This is what we are also called to do as Christians pursuing obedience to God's call. We are to remain diligent in the dark, in the times when things feel hard or unclear or when we feel unseen. No matter the difficulty and uncertainty you might be walking through, God is at work within and through you.

Don't let spiritual setbacks hold you back from taking Spirit-led risks and honoring God in everything you do. The all-surpassing power of God dwells within you (yes, you), and His power is made evident through you. What a relief it is to know that our goodness doesn't qualify us to be used for His righteousness. Matter of fact, it's the opposite.

You might not feel like you have what it takes to be used by God. Sister, nothing could be further from the truth. All you need is what you have in hand, a willing heart, and Christ within you. Today's a good day to believe in the all-surpassing power of God at work within you. Take a step forward in obedience and let the Lord take care of the rest.

REFLECTION QUESTIONS

1. When has a significant shift or "sharp turn" in your life led to unexpected growth or discovery in your personal journey?

2. Reflecting on Cass's leap into writing during a time of uncertainty, when have you felt called to step out in faith without clear foresight of the outcome?

3. Can you identify a small step of obedience you've taken recently? How does it align with the larger mission or purpose you feel called to?

4. How do you navigate and grow from the trials and "dark nights of the soul" in a way that deepens your faith and resilience?

EIGHT

BREAKING UP
WITH IDLENESS

Psalm 1:3 paints a vivid image of a tree planted by streams of water, flourishing and yielding fruit in season. This tree represents a vibrant spiritual life, deeply rooted in faith and God's Word. But if I'm (Britt) being totally honest, I've also felt like a different kind of tree at times, one seemingly stuck in an eternal winter, barren and without signs of life. That was the state of my spirit during one of the most challenging phases of my life.

I don't know if you're like me, but sometimes I look back at significant moments of my life and see them as a movie playing in my head. In the reel of my memories, one specific, spiritually dormant period painfully stands out. Due to my lack of diligence in pursuing Jesus during that season, the fire of my passion for Him and for living purposefully dimmed to a mere flicker. I forgot who I was in Him. I got caught up in the busyness of changing my location and starting a new marriage at the tender age of twenty-three.

I'll be blunt. This period looked like a whole lot of me being a lazy couch potato and taking only three hundred steps a day, getting up only to go to the bathroom and the kitchen. I've told this story in previous books but not nearly to this extent or detail, and it's because there's a different kind of truth to unpack here. Something I missed until now.

Life in Indiana (where my husband and I had moved after getting married) seemed a world away from everything familiar and comfortable to me. It was an illustration of solitude: no friends, no family, no church. While my sweet husband stood as a constant pillar of support and prayer, an inexplicable loneliness permeated my being. At the same time, the weight of responsibility I felt as a young wife, coupled with the effects of my upbringing where a godly marriage was uncharted territory, rendered me motionless and scared. I felt vulnerable and inadequate. I rarely sought guidance or mentorship, which I now know is so important. Instead, I navigated life's difficulties solely on survival instincts. And my survival instincts led me nowhere, as the only goal was to survive.

In biblical history, we can find many moments that reflect these same struggles with accepting responsibility and change. For example, let's take a look at Saul. Saul was Israel's first king. When it was time for him to be presented to the people of Israel after being anointed king by the prophet Samuel, Saul was nowhere to be found. Instead of stepping into his new role with boldness, grace, and reliance upon the Lord, he hid himself among the baggage. The weight of his impending kingship and the sheer magnitude of his new responsibilities overwhelmed him. I mean, I get it. Big responsibility tends to make me a little skittish too.

This scene from 1 Samuel 10:22 offers us a glimpse into Saul's heart—his hesitation, his apprehension, and perhaps even his sense of unworthiness. Like many of us, Saul wrestled with the fear of embracing what God had set before him. It's a powerful reminder that, even in the face of His purpose, we can sometimes shrink back and become stagnant and complacent, daunted by the challenges and responsibilities ahead. But the Lord is faithful and patient.

Often our hesitation to embrace God's calling mirrors our natural instincts when faced with threats or unexpected challenges in the physical world. Most of you are probably familiar with the fight-or-flight response. This reaction readies us either to face a perceived threat boldly or to quickly escape from it. But what many might not realize is that our bodies sometimes engage in other reactions, such as "freeze" and "fawn."

I am not a licensed therapist or psychiatrist, but I've found that understanding the ways our brains and bodies are wired casts light on our spiritual behaviors as well. So I'm sharing a tool I learned in therapy that has blessed me in many ways. Let me break it down for you.

There are four main trauma responses, which I'll list below:

- **Fight:** When escape isn't viable, you might decide to confront the danger directly. This might manifest as thinking, *If I can't escape the lion in my path, I'll have to fight it.*
- **Flight:** This response is about escaping danger. If you were responding with the instinct toward flight, you'd think, *I need to run away and distance myself from this threat.*
- **Freeze:** Here, the body and mind essentially play dead. It's like shutting down in the face of peril, unable to decide or act, hoping the lion might ignore a seemingly lifeless being.
- **Fawn:** This is perhaps the most nuanced of the responses. It's about appeasing the threat. In this scenario, one might think, *If I can't fight or flee from the lion, perhaps I can keep it calm and content.* This response is often seen in individuals with people-pleasing tendencies.

I have come to learn that my default response to overwhelming situations, particularly those that blend responsibility with fear, is to freeze. I want to clarify: It wasn't marriage itself that triggered this response all those years ago; rather, it was the immense fear I felt of failing at it. So, on many of those days, 12:00 p.m. became my normal wake-up time. Wearing the same T-shirt I had on the day before, I would sluggishly drag my feet to the kitchen. With every step weighed down by a mix of melancholy and apathy, I'd brew myself a pot of coffee with my eyes half open and then settle into the all-too-familiar embrace of my couch, losing myself in the endless binge of Netflix shows. All. Day. Long.

As evening approached, a sense of dread would start to build within me. The soft click of a key turning in the lock, signaling my husband's return, would shoot a pang of guilt and embarrassment into my heart. How could I let him see me this way—seemingly unchanged from how he'd left me in the morning? He was out in the world, facing it, working tirelessly for our future, while I remained trapped in an endless loop of lethargy, fearful of facing anything, let alone the world. Other than short trips to the grocery store, this was pretty much my life for almost a year.

In that year, I didn't grow. I remained stagnant, idle. I was in a frozen, barren state. Maybe you've been in a similar place?

The biblical story of Elijah resonates deeply for me here. After his triumphant showdown at Mount Carmel, Elijah found himself fleeing for his life, sinking into despair, and ultimately taking refuge in a cave (1 Kings 19). It was a stark contrast to the prophet who had just witnessed fire coming down from heaven. In his solitude and fear, Elijah believed he was alone, much like I felt in Indiana.

But God showed up for Elijah in that cave. Not in the mighty wind, the earthquake, or the fire, but in a gentle whisper, reminding Elijah that he wasn't alone.

For me, Indiana was my personal cave of desolation, leading to a spiritual paralysis I thought I could never break out of. Each day blurred into the next: waking up late, wearing yesterday's clothes, the steady sound of Netflix filling the void of silence. On one such day, settled into my customary spot, I experienced a sudden awakening from my idle slumber. It was as if I was jolted awake. It felt like I had been yanked right out of the Matrix, becoming acutely aware of the destructiveness of my behavior—to myself, to my relationship with Jesus, and to my marriage.

It brought to mind Adam Sandler's movie *Click*. In it, Sandler's character uses a remote to fast-forward through life, but in doing so, he ends up on autopilot, merely existing. His fervent wish to skip the mundane costs him dearly, and he ends up with a faltering marriage and strained ties with his children. He misses the beauty of the *now*.

In my moment of clarity, it felt like the Lord pressed pause for me just to grant me this insight. And I'll never forget, I heard the Lord whisper to my heart so gently, *One day, you will share about this time in your life, and it will deeply resonate with others.* But then, as swiftly as this revelation came, I found myself shaking it off, like I was emerging from a vivid daydream and then immediately reverting back to my stagnant state.

But the seed was planted after I heard His whisper. Maybe I didn't act on it right away, but it ignited something in me.

EMERGING FROM MY CAVE

I (Britt) will never forget the day I felt the Lord speak to me to move and to get myself unstuck. I had finally reached a breaking point, weary of living life on autopilot, just drifting through the days without intention or purpose. I was quite literally fed up with myself. I knew something needed to change.

Throughout this phase, my husband was an unwavering anchor, a living testament to patience and loyalty. The Lord, through him, highlighted the true essence of faithfulness. One evening, as we fluffed our pillows across the bed from each other, I softly approached the topic of seeking employment.

"I think it's time for me to get a job and get myself out of this."

Tears flooded my husband's eyes as he shared that he had been fervently praying for me to find that very spark, to finally allow myself to be rooted somewhere new.

For me, securing a job wasn't just about working. It symbolized something far greater and far more meaningful in my wintered state. It signified establishing ties and planting myself. Finally getting up off the couch and facing the world. Facing my marriage. Facing my relationship with the Lord. Waking up from idleness and living in diligence.

It wasn't easy for me to realize the state I was in wasn't healthy. While lounging on the couch day in and day out might seem comfortable and effortless, comfort does not always equate to vitality and well-being. Like the Lord whispered to Elijah in that cave, He whispered to me in my dark place, and I was willing to listen and obey.

Stagnation and idleness don't necessarily look the same for everyone. They manifest differently for each believer at different times in different seasons for different reasons. If you feel you could be living in stagnation, know that you are not alone. It's a lot more common than it seems. Especially in our scrolling-obsessed culture. Life is hard and messy, and we are constantly under spiritual attack. Sometimes it's easy to check out and numb out. And when we do, the spiritual attack we're under isn't always evident. The subtle, little decisions made over the course of time can get us stuck.

Here are some stagnation scenarios that might resonate with your walk.

- **Procrastination.** Perhaps God has placed a mission or purpose in your heart, but out of fear or doubt, you've been delaying your obedience. Recurrently saying "I'll start tomorrow" can be an indication that you're not heeding His voice.
- **Reluctance to Leave the Familiar.** God often calls us to step outside of our comfort zone, much like He did with Abraham and Moses. If you are clinging to old habits, environments, or relationships that no longer align with God's purpose for you, it might be a form of spiritual stagnation.
- **Overthinking.** While it's wise to always seek God's guidance and wisdom, endlessly overthinking without taking steps of faith and obedience can prevent you from stepping into what He is calling you to do.
- **Avoiding Spiritual Depth.** Perhaps you're shying away from deep prayer, reflection, or addressing past hurts that need His healing. Surface-level faith, without deepening your relationship with Christ, can lead to spiritual idleness.

- **Routine Without Renewal.** Daily devotions and prayers are essential, but if every day feels ritualistic without a renewed sense of God's presence, it might signal a plateau in your spiritual growth.
- **Waiting Without Wisdom.** Sometimes, God does ask us to wait. There is so much beauty to behold in waiting, so much to learn in those periods. But perpetual waiting without seeking His guidance or having a readiness to move when He says to move can leave you feeling stuck. Waiting without drawing wisdom from the Lord can often lead to not participating.
- **Staying Busy.** While productivity is a good thing, it can sometimes mask deeper issues. Constant busyness might be a subtle way of escaping emotional or spiritual confrontations, preventing you from laying your burdens before Jesus. This isn't just about avoiding spiritual depth; it's about subconsciously distracting yourself from facing the healing that Christ offers.

If any of these sound like you and you've been holding off on growing and pursuing any kind of purpose He has for you, we want to help you reclaim the vitality of your faith again. We want to help you emerge from whatever cave you are in, face the world again, and fan into flame the passion in your heart for Jesus like never before.

We pray that as you read these words He would restore to you the joy of your salvation, the joy you once felt when you said yes to Jesus and gave Him your heart forever. We pray that joy be reignited in your heart once more, right now.

THE COST OF STAGNATION

Each of us on our spiritual journey will face moments where we feel trapped, stagnant, or distant from the Lord. My (Britt's) own encounter with this was a poignant chapter of my life, marked by idleness and a numbing sense of mere existence rather than a vibrant, active faith in Christ. Honestly, I think we all get stuck there at times. I still find myself going through periods like this every now and then, but I'm thankful that I now have tools that can get me out of it through the working power of the Holy Spirit.

It's crucial to recognize that the Enemy is always lurking, seeking opportunities to divert and undermine God's purpose for our lives. When he can't obliterate us, he strategizes to side-track God's plans for us. Sometimes even by causing us to be immovable.

Emerging from my own season of stagnation was a challenging endeavor, because the comfort of escaping my problems was seductive. But I learned that when we choose avoidance—when we freeze instead of facing adversity head-on—we miss out on the healing that comes from laying our burdens at Jesus' feet. I won't dwell on this, but I can't help but wonder how many months and years I've wasted by living in hiding, paralyzed by fear of failure and the weight of responsibility.

Whether the stagnation you're facing is brought on or triggered by perceived threat or stress, it's something that can be quite costly.

I don't know about you, but I don't want to reach the end of my life and come face-to-face with Jesus and have Him show me all the things He could have done through my life had I not let fear and laziness hold me back. I'm baring my soul here because I long for you to not have to fight such battles for as long as I did. I long for you to break out of whatever spiritual paralysis you find yourself in so you can experience the fullness of what He has for you, friend.

Remember that while we might be stationary in our faith at times, true growth is about choosing to move forward, even when faced with adversity, challenges, or fear. For me, the path to freedom required a deep introspection, guided by earnest prayer and the discernment offered by the Holy Spirit. Whatever that looks like for you, please don't waste any more time getting on that path. Time is something we don't get back.

Now that we've touched on what spiritual stagnation is and how to identify it, let's take a look at how to break out of it.

WALKING IN DILIGENCE

If you've ever felt caught in the stillness of spiritual idleness, with your spiritual fire barely an ember, you're not alone. As you know already, I've been there, and many others have too.

It's sort of like being at a spiritual intersection, isn't it? On one side, there's the familiar comfort of simply doing nothing, just letting life glide by. But on the other side? There's diligence, this beautiful, energetic pursuit of a deeper relationship with our Creator.

When I think of a life lived in diligence, seeking the things of the Lord, I see it as a beautifully sunlit path that is marked by His will and by our willingness to walk down it. The Bible teaches us that those who passionately seek the Lord find immeasurable rewards. He rewards those who diligently seek Him (Hebrews 11:6).

But what happens when our seeking becomes a bit . . . lackluster? Our walk with Jesus isn't just a yes and a direct shot to heaven with no struggle or challenge. No, the reality is sin exists and we have an enemy. And the enemy of our souls uses people, situations, traumas—you name it—to pull us from Jesus. Seeking Jesus with devotion is like tending a garden. Some days the weeds of distraction and disinterest will creep in. We will face struggles, doubts, and uncertainties. We will go through periods of feeling like we're in the wilderness. And what happens when the zeal we once lived with starts to dissipate? We start to drift or wander, letting days blur into one another, missing out on the opportunity to use our God-given talents, time, and treasures.

Let's step onto that sunlit path together, friend. How? First, let's take a closer look at the definitions of diligence and idleness.

Diligence is more than just effort. It's a consistent, earnest, and energetic effort in one's pursuits, especially in obeying God's Word and seeking His wisdom. At its core, diligence is about giving our utmost to God and being unwaveringly faithful, even in the minutiae of life. The rewards diligence offers are many, such as spiritual growth, fruitfulness, and a strengthened faith.

Think of your spiritual life as a garden. As you nurture it with prayer, study, and action, you're not just going through the motions. You're connecting with God, learning about His will, and applying His Word to your life. That's how you grow, bit by bit, day by day. And here's the thing about growth—it's not always visible right away, but with consistent care, your spiritual life will flourish and bear fruit that can only come from living close to God.

Now, fruitfulness isn't just about what you produce; it's a sign of life, of vitality. When you are diligent in your faith, you are actively participating in God's work, and that brings a vibrancy to everything you do. You become someone who not only talks about faith but lives it out so vividly that others can't help but notice.

But what about the flip side—idleness? Contrary to simple inactivity, spiritual idleness is a stagnation that speaks to a deeper lack of purpose, commitment, and zeal for God. It's the silent erosion of passion, leading believers into the quicksand of complacency.

Spiritual idleness is like neglecting your garden. It's not about being still; it's wasting the opportunity to live fully for

CONTRARY TO SIMPLE INACTIVITY, SPIRITUAL IDLENESS IS A STAGNATION THAT SPEAKS TO A DEEPER LACK OF PURPOSE, COMMITMENT, AND ZEAL FOR GOD. IT'S THE SILENT EROSION OF PASSION, LEADING BELIEVERS INTO THE QUICKSAND OF COMPLACENCY.

God. That can slowly start to pull you away from the vibrant life God has planned for you. When we're idle, we miss out on so many moments to experience God and to serve Him. Our faith regresses.

Picture a boat that's not anchored: it doesn't stay in one place; it drifts away. That's what happens to us when we're spiritually idle. We drift, and that leaves us vulnerable. We're not only vulnerable to temptation but also to losing our discernment and our ability to recognize God's voice and His leading.

We break out of idleness by living in diligence. It's a daily decision we each have to make. So if you have struggled or are struggling with spiritual stagnation, the answer for how to free yourself from your idle state is to seek the Lord with diligence. What does that look like? Here are some steps you can take to cultivate a diligent heart.

- **Ignite the Desire.** Recognize the desire within you to pursue God more earnestly. Like any deep relationship, it starts with a yearning. If you haven't ignited that desire yet, ask the Holy Spirit to awaken that desire. It all begins with an inner hunger for God. This isn't about routine or ritual, but an intense craving to know Him more intimately. Ask yourself: *Do I desire God above all else?* Let this be the foundation of your pursuit.

- **Prioritize Time with Him.** You can't know someone intimately without spending time with them. Regularly study His Word. Don't just read the words. Study them. Meditate on them. Unpack them. Even if you're just reading the same verse over and over again, try to understand it in every possible way you can so you can apply it to your life. And let His Word not only be something you know but something you live. It should be a source of nourishment, not just knowledge.

- **Pray Vulnerably.** Have you ever had vulnerable conversations with someone? Conversations where you pour out your heart and empty yourself with the hope that the other person will see you, understand you, and even possibly give you advice or instruction on how to deal with whatever problem you are facing? Do that with God. Speak aloud what's in your heart. Approach God with raw honesty, laying out your fears, hopes, regrets, and desires. It's in this vulnerable space with Him that deep intimacy is built.

- **Exalt the Father Through Worship.** In the gospel of Matthew, Jesus offered a profound lesson on how to approach our heavenly Father in prayer. Often referred to as "The Lord's Prayer," it begins with, "Our Father in heaven, hallowed be your name" (6:9). You see, before any petition or request, Jesus placed the emphasis on glorifying the Father. This isn't just an introduction; it's a posture. True worship is about elevating God, acknowledging His majesty, and recalling His boundless goodness. So, the next time you pray, start by lifting His name above all else. In this space of adoration, you'll find immense closeness to His presence.

- **Surrender Continuously.** Every day, surrender your plans, ambitions, and desires to God. Diligence isn't a one-time decision, but a daily choice to prioritize His will over yours.

Here's what I'd love for you to ponder: How are you tending to your spiritual garden? Are there areas where you have been diligent and you can see the growth and fruit that have come from it? Are there patches that have been neglected, where idleness has crept in? Think about the steps you can take today to reengage with God, dig your hands into the soil of faith, and get back to diligently tending your garden, ready for what God has in store. Life with Him is always moving forward, and there's always more to discover.

DILIGENCE IS A BY-PRODUCT OF REVERENCE

I (Britt) walked into my home church on a Sunday morning more than a decade ago, eager to worship Jesus. I was just a baby Christian then. I'll never forget the beautiful windows of this church. The ceiling was a harmonious mix of high beams and sun-welcoming windows. The sun shone so brightly into the lobby that it practically kissed my skin with warmth. It felt like one big giant hug from God every Sunday morning. When I walked through those doors, I would look up and smile. Then I'd grab a cup of coffee sweetened with my usual two shots of French vanilla creamer. Routinely, I'd set my Bible on the table, stir my coffee, smile at the guest services team, then clutch both my Bible and my coffee and head into the auditorium to fetch my seat.

That particular Sunday, as I was fixing my coffee, someone gently grabbed my arm. "Hey, Brittany! I'd love to chat for a minute if you have time before the service!" It was Simone. Simone was a vibrant beacon of faith and zeal. Her life was deeply intertwined with this warm, sun-kissed church we both called home. With a gentle demeanor, she was just as kind as you could imagine. I was so happy to have someone my age to talk to. The conversation that followed is one I still reflect on, one filled with her passion for Jesus and my own bubbling, growing desire for Him. A quick heart-to-heart that I'll forever treasure and remember.

As I shared my story with her, recounting my path to finding Jesus, the compassion behind her eyes stood out to me. We sat at one of the high bistro-style tables off to the right of the lobby, and there was that warm sun again, glowing on us as we had this conversation. Simone cared. She leaned forward as she listened intently. She empathized with where I had been and encouraged me toward where I was going. We had never had a conversation before this, but I knew who she was and I looked up to her. As you can imagine, I was feeling so blessed!

As she continued to listen with compassion, the sermon began. We both looked at the auditorium and realized we had gotten lost in conversation. Her parting words for me were, "Keep that fire alive, Britt. Don't let that fire in you for Him burn out."

I smiled, and said, "I won't. I promise."

Inwardly I replied with, *How* could *I let this fire burn out? The love I feel for Him is so intense; how could it ever wane?*

"Life happens, and sometimes things get in the way," she said, almost as if she was giving an answer to my inward question without my vocalizing it.

As more than a decade has passed, I've come to understand the weight of Simone's words. That spiritual fervor, that initial blaze, can indeed diminish if not tended to, if not fed and nurtured. Sadly, it did for me. Not a badge of pride I'm happy to wear. I broke my promise to Simone. I unknowingly, unintentionally let the fire burn out.

In my efforts to reignite the flame of my faith, Hebrews 12:28–29 has sort of become my flashlight in the fog. It speaks about our worship with reverence, saying it should be a reflection of our awe and deep respect for Him.

My life and perspective of God changed drastically when I learned about the word *reverence*. Do me a favor and grab a highlighter and highlight that word.

That word jumps out at me each time I see it, prompting a deep dive into what it really means and how to live in it. Reverence is about deep respect and awe. Think about someone you deeply respect. You hang on their every word, cherish your time with them, and give them your full attention.

In the Old Testament, reverence combined this awe-inspiring respect (*yare'*) with actions that show honor (*shachah*). It's like that feeling of being small against the vastness of the ocean, but in the best way. It's the overwhelming sense of something bigger than us. And we show that respect through our actions.

But here's the thing. Our modern world doesn't really get this whole reverence deal. We're all about doing things fast and moving on to the next big thing. Very seldom do we slow down and take in our own awe of God.

But if we're talking about following Him with everything we've got, about breaking out of stagnation and pursuing diligence toward His calling, it has to start with pausing and letting this deep-seated respect for Him seep in. And then you'll come to notice how it changes how you approach everything in life. Your actions, decisions—they all start flowing out of this place of wanting to honor Him because you're in awe of who He is.

I can't help but see the comparison here to the verse, "He must increase, but I must decrease" (John 3:30). That's not to say we must lower ourselves and think less of ourselves. Instead, we are to think of ourselves less and put Him above all. There's power in putting Him above everything else, even when our flesh wants to be first.

So, when Proverbs 9:10 talks about the fear of the Lord being the beginning of wisdom, it's not necessarily about being scared or frightened. No, it's a jaw-dropping awe and respect that beckons us closer to Him and pushes us to live our lives in a way that shows respect and honor for Him in all that we do.

Long story short, reverence changed the game for me. It turned my faith from being about just going through the motions to this vibrant, living thing. It's almost like putting on glasses and seeing the world in HD for the first time. Suddenly, everything is brighter, clearer, and you just can't help but want to live in a way that shows off this amazing God you serve and love.

So, friend, if you're like me and wondering how to keep that fire burning bright, start with reverence. This isn't about adding more to your spiritual to-do list, but rather seeing Him for who He truly is. Let the awe and respect fill you up, and then let everything else overflow from that place.

THE JOURNEY TOWARD CONSISTENCY

I (Britt) have a confession to make, just between us. Every January 1 of the last five years, I've whispered a promise to myself: "This will be the year of consistency for me." Consistency in drawing closer to Jesus, eating healthier, staying active, and so on. My goal has been to break out of the stagnation I find myself in time and time again. But, if I'm laying it all out there,

I've stumbled every single time, almost right out of the gate. Why is consistency so hard for me?

At this point in my thirty-three years of living, I genuinely do not understand why I struggle to stay consistent. The number of times I've begun a new habit, only to watch it fade away into nothing, is, well, more than I'd like to admit out loud. And the impact? It's there, in the mirror, in each out-of-breath step up the stairs, in the corners of my heart where I realize I haven't been as present with Jesus as I long to be. Binge-watching *The Office* every night while eating snacks probably hasn't served me well either. I do want to clarify—earlier when we talked about leisure activities being okay, they are. But when they get in the way of our progress and growth, they're probably not great.

So, why *is* consistency such a difficult thing to attain? I think there could be several different answers. But here's a thought, maybe even an answer, one that's starting to take root as I type these words and share this with you. Maybe it's not so much about being able to do more of the same thing over and over (consistency). Maybe it's about replacing our old ways with something infinitely better, little by little. Small by small. In increments.

For example, I get super overwhelmed with laundry and dishes. They have a way of turning into mini-mountains in my house. And let me tell you, they definitely don't just sit there looking pretty. They grow—oh boy, do they grow—like they're competing for some kind of Mount Everest of Household Chores award. And as they ascend higher and higher, my motivation descends lower and lower.

I think part of the problem is my approach. I have this knack for seeing these tasks in their full, daunting glory. You'd think the stress of seeing them would kick my butt into gear to take care of them, but it does the opposite. Hello, procrastination! Blame it on me having ADHD or maybe just a misguided sense of adventure. I mean, who looks at a sink full of dishes and thinks, *Ah, yes, one gigantic task. Perfect!*? But really, what helps me to eventually tackle this mountain of a task is doing it little by little and thinking of it as such. One dish at a time, one load at a time.

James Clear hit the nail on the head in his *New York Times* bestselling book *Atomic Habits*:

> A slight change in your daily habits can guide your life to a very different destination. Making a choice that is 1 percent better or 1 percent worse seems insignificant in the moment, but over the span of moments that make up a lifetime these choices determine the difference between who you are and who you could be.[1]

Now, obviously, there's not much you could add to the process of doing dishes to make it feel like you're building a better thing into your life. At the end of the day, dishes are dishes, and they need to be done. But my point is for us to remember that the little by little is actually not so little. We need to change our perspective.

What if we look at consistency differently? What if we see it as a journey of diligent pursuit and not another mountain that needs to be tackled? Then, it's not about the mundane repetition of tasks, which, I'll be honest, tremendously overwhelms me. Instead, it becomes a vibrant, living quest. A chance to actively chase something.

This journey toward consistency isn't just effort for effort's sake. It's a pursuit that is alive, filled with purpose and direction. And the most beautiful part? The reward we find at the end is Jesus. He is the greatest reward of all.

The opposite of this journey toward consistency would be keeping ourselves trapped in idleness while the mountain before us just keeps getting higher and higher. Through the years, I've realized the difficulty of being consistent isn't so much about the discomfort of having to do the same thing over and over again, but that I lose momentum fast. And the reason that happens is because something is missing. I haven't really addressed the root of the problem.

Let's unpack this for a moment with some Scripture. David prayed, "Create in me a clean heart, O God, and renew a right spirit within me" (Psalm 51:10). Reading this sparks a thought in me that maybe my struggles with consistency are a matter of my heart not being right, that perhaps my devotion needs realigning. Are my daily efforts a genuine offering to the Lord, or are they just items on a checklist in an attempt to accomplish consistency? Just as Jesus spoke of the greatest commandment to "love the Lord your God with all your heart and with all your soul and with all your mind" (Matthew 22:37), I'm learning that my actions need to stem from this pure place of wholehearted love and devotion.

The scary thing? It hasn't always. There have been many times, more than I'd like to admit, when my actions were more about going through the motions than a true expression of love for God. Times when I became complacent rather than consistent in pursuing Him. It's a sobering realization, really, confronting the fact that my heart at times hasn't been fully in sync with my endeavors.

EACH DAY PRESENTS A FRESH OPPORTUNITY FOR REALIGNMENT, FOR STEERING OUR HEARTS BACK TOWARD GOD.

But here's where grace and growth intertwine, friend. Each day presents a fresh opportunity for realignment, for steering our hearts back toward God. It's about more than just adhering to a routine; it's about anchoring each action in pure devotion. What would it look like to truly give Him all of our devotion?

I don't know about you, but when my day begins with seeking Him, everything else falls into place—not perfectly, but purposefully.

REFLECTION QUESTIONS

1. Think of a time when fear of a new responsibility led to avoidance rather than action. How did you eventually face the challenge?

2. How have you experienced the freeze response in your spiritual life, and what strategy helped you to move forward and reengage with your faith?

3. When have you encountered spiritual stagnation, and what specific actions reignited your diligence in pursuing Jesus?

4. Why do you think consistency in spiritual practices is challenging? Share strategies that have helped you maintain daily diligence in your faith walk.

WHAT PURPOSE IS THERE IN THIS VERY MOMENT?

Have you ever had one of those moments when you're so focused on the destination that you forget about the journey? I know I (Britt) have. Especially when it comes to understanding our purpose on this side of heaven. Many of us, including myself, have often thought of purpose as this big, final destination we're all trying to reach. But then what?

Picture this example: A young woman named Rosie has always dreamed of climbing Mount Everest. It's been on her bucket list since she was a child. Every time she closes her eyes, she imagines that moment of triumph, standing at the peak, looking out at the world below. The dream is so vivid, so powerful, that it consumes her every thought.

To make this dream a reality, Rosie starts to train. She's

in the gym day in and day out, lifting weights, running on the treadmill, preparing her body for the strenuous climb. She spends thousands of dollars on the best gear, reads every book on mountain climbing, and even takes altitude-training classes.

When the big day finally arrives, Rosie begins her ascent. But as she's climbing, she's so laser-focused on reaching the top that she fails to notice the beauty around her. The intricate ice formations, the breathtaking views, the togetherness among fellow climbers, the thrill of each goal reached, and even the lessons from the challenges she faces—these all seem to her to be mere obstacles or distractions from her ultimate goal.

By the time Rosie reaches the peak, she's exhausted and overwhelmed. Yes, she's achieved her dream, but the moment feels sort of . . . empty. In her singular focus on the destination, she has missed out on the richness of the journey. She realizes the climb itself, with all its ups and downs, was the real adventure. The relationships made, the personal growth experienced, and the simple moments of awe at God's creation were the true treasures of her quest, not just the final panoramic view from the top.

Our point here? It's easy to become so enamored with our Everest, our end goal, that we overlook the value and beauty to behold along the way. What does God have for us, in this very moment, that He doesn't want us to overlook?

Rosie's story reminds me a lot about our walk with Christ. Just like Rosie was so caught up in reaching the peak of Everest that she missed the beauty of the climb, we, too, can get so wrapped up in our broader purpose or end goal that we overlook the precious daily moments with Jesus along the way.

IT'S EASY TO BECOME SO ENAMORED WITH OUR EVEREST, OUR END GOAL, THAT WE OVERLOOK THE VALUE AND BEAUTY TO BEHOLD ALONG THE WAY.

In Matthew 25, Jesus told the parable of the ten bridesmaids. To give you a quick recap, ten bridesmaids were waiting for a bridegroom. Half of them were super prepared and brought extra oil for their lamps, but the other half? Eh, not so much. And when the bridegroom took a tad longer than expected to arrive, those without the extra oil were in a real pickle. Their lamps started going out, and when they went to get more oil, they missed the whole celebration.

Why am I talking about bridesmaids and lamps? Well, it hit me that this story isn't just about *being* ready; it's about *staying* ready. And when I think about Rosie's journey up Everest, I can't help but see parallels with the story of the ten bridesmaids. Rosie was so consumed and fixated on reaching the peak that she missed the beauty of every step leading to it. Likewise, those bridesmaids who ran out of oil were probably so fixated on the big event—the arrival of the bridegroom—that they neglected their immediate responsibility of keeping their lamps filled with oil so they didn't burn out.

Let's take a moment and connect these dots. Rosie's journey teaches us the importance of embracing every part of our journey, not just the end point. And the bridesmaids? They are a stark reminder that our relationship with Jesus isn't about one grand gesture or waiting for one defining moment. It's about daily devotion, preparation, and commitment.

Imagine if Rosie had treasured each step, each sunrise. And picture those bridesmaids if they'd realized their duty wasn't just to wait but to actively prepare. Both scenarios essentially teach us the same lesson: It's the daily choices, the now, that matters. The small acts of faith lead us to what is greater.

Purpose is not always a far-off destination. It's not really an endgame. It's now. It's in the everyday, in every act of devotion, every moment of obedience, every prayer, every expression of love. In the wise words of our friend Hope Harris, "Purpose doesn't pause."[1] If we want to be active in pursuing our purpose, we need to be engaged in the continual process of devoting ourselves to Christ with diligence.

Think of it this way. Just as Rosie needed to appreciate every step of her climb, we need to treasure every day we are given, filling our lamps with fresh oil, readying ourselves for Christ's return. It's not enough to rely on yesterday's oil or past deeds.

I love this quote by Mark Batterson:

The only way to be fully alive is to be fully present, and the only way to be fully present is to live in day-tight compartments. For far too many of us, life feels like the meaningless passage of time between far too few meaningful moments. And even when they do come along, we take selfies instead of being fully present. We miss the moment because we're living in the wrong time zone. We're so fixated on the past and so anxious about the future that we miss the present. Then we wonder where life went.[2]

You see, friend, each day offers a new chance, a new moment to engage with our faith and grow closer to Him, and to participate in His purpose for us right now. What would it look like to start embracing today without pining for yesterday or being anxious about tomorrow? How can we keep our oil lamps filled and ready? Here are a few suggestions.

- **Find Nourishment in His Word.** Just like a warm, comforting meal, let the Bible be your daily sustenance. Time in His Word every day can be like a daily hug from God, reminding you of His presence and love.
- **Talk to God Anytime, Anywhere.** Imagine God as your closest friend who is always right beside you. Share your thoughts, worries, fears, joys, and even the mundane details of your day with Him through prayer.
- **Lean into Community.** Surround yourself with people who radiate God's love. Whether it's a weekly Bible study, a heartfelt chat over coffee, or a prayer-group thread on social media, these connections can refuel your soul.
- **Worship in the Mundane.** Worship isn't just for Sundays. Find moments of worship in your daily routines—it could be praising God while doing chores or admiring His handiwork in nature. Worship isn't just about music.

- **Reflect and Realign.** Regularly take stock of your spiritual health. Are there areas of your life that need realignment? Sometimes, keeping our lamp filled means trimming the wick—removing things that hinder our spiritual growth.

In the rush of life, it can be hard to remember that God's love is a constant source of strength. But we want to encourage you, friend. Keeping your spiritual lamp filled isn't about doing more; it's about deepening your relationship with Him, even in the little things. In the now.

DON'T LOOK BACK

So, you might be asking, *What if I have wasted time? What if I haven't lived each day on purpose? What if I'm stuck, fixating on yesterday?* If you're anything like me (Britt), you've probably done this a lot. It's hard, because we want to learn from the past but we don't want to get stuck there in our minds. If we aren't careful, we can end up residing in what's gone on before without embracing the beauty in the now. While memories and aspirations are an essential part of living, it's crucial to recognize that true living—Christ-centered, purposeful living—happens in the present, as we've stated above. For it is here, in the present, that we find the raw material for kingdom living.

A while back, I went through a season with my daughter that

taught me an important lesson about being present and active in the now. To all the mamas: You know those toddler days when your little one will only nap on you and not in their bed? Yes, the notorious contact naps. As much as I cherished these snuggly moments, they came with a challenge. I found it very tough to sit my antsy ADHD butt still for a couple of hours each day, especially with a to-do list that seemed to grow by the minute—dishes waiting, laundry piling up, dinner to be prepped, and so on.

During this contact-nap phase, I found myself craving uninterrupted quiet time with God. I prayed and prayed and prayed for time alone with Him, where I could just find the peace to be still. It's hard to get that as a mama. My husband and I joked about all the free time we used to have before becoming parents. In a way, I longed for those days. All I wanted was at least twenty minutes to read the Word and pray without my mind buzzing around like a busy bumblebee. But every time I tried to sneak away and put my daughter down in her bed, it was like she had this sixth sense. The moment her head left my chest, those big, beautiful brown eyes would pop open, and she'd start crying.

So there I was, back in that cozy corner of her bedroom, rocking back and forth on her soft rocking chair, feeling a mixture of love and frustration. Maybe more than a tinge, though. *When will I ever get a moment to myself?* I wondered. It felt like I was in this never-ending phase where personal space and time were distant memories. But then, in that quiet rocking chair, I heard something that changed everything. A gentle whisper in my heart said, *Maybe this is your time to be still before Me.* It hit me like a warm summer breeze. Not only did He answer my prayer, but He gave me something else to cherish while having that quiet time—my daughter lying on my chest. I had prayed to be a mama, prayed for these moments. God had answered my prayers, and I was living in an answered prayer.

This wasn't just about naps or chores. This was an invitation to embrace stillness, to see the opportunity I did have in my present, to turn these moments into sacred time with Him. I grabbed my phone (thank God for the Bible App by YouVersion) and started soaking up Scripture while my daughter rested peacefully in my arms.

Day by day, this became our routine. And I started to really look forward to it. Her breaths, soft and rhythmic against me, became the soundtrack to my prayer and Bible study time. It was a season of unexpected blessings, a lesson in finding God in the stillness of life's simplest, most mundane moments. I realized the present was just the next step in the same journey I had always been on.

During that season, Scripture struck a chord with me, and I found a parable that reinforced the idea of not looking back but keeping our eyes on what is in front of us, what we've been given for today. It was the one where Jesus talked about the importance of keeping our hand on the plow. Luke 9:62 seemed to leap off the page at me: "No one who puts his hand to the plow and looks back is fit for the kingdom of God." What was Jesus talking about here, and why did it stay with me so long?

I'll be completely transparent with you: Those words

initially sent a shiver down my spine. I stared at the words on my phone screen while rocking my daughter back and forth, feeling like I wanted to sit at the edge of my chair in suspense as I took them in. The words "not fit for the kingdom of God" felt like a very sobering warning about the consequences of what I do with my time. The beauty of this challenging scripture is that it's not just about the times we falter or step away from our calling. It's about what we do next.

This verse holds an important and transforming message for anyone seeking purpose in the present without pining for yesterday. It's more than just a farming analogy; it's a life principle. It beckons us to dive deeper into the significance of embracing today and following Jesus right now.

Let me break down for you what exactly this verse means, agriculturally speaking. Understanding Scripture from a historical and cultural context helps us gain the perspective we need to apply it to our lives. The plow in this verse is a tool that was used to turn over the earth, break it up, and prepare it for planting. The plow's purpose was to make the hard, compacted soil receptive to seeds, enabling growth and eventually a fruitful harvest.

Operating a plow in these ancient times was no simple task. It required strength, focus, and precision. The person plowing would grip the handles with their hands and push forward, while an animal, often an ox, pulled it. The plowman had to maintain constant pressure and direction to plow a straight line. If the plowman were to get distracted and take his hand off the plow, the path would become crooked, making the task of planting and harvesting much more challenging and ineffective. In today's terms, it could look like taking your hand off a steering wheel while looking behind you. What would happen? Well, I'm sure you can imagine.

Jesus was painting a vivid picture His listeners would have immediately understood. To put one's hand to the plow was to commit to a task that required undivided attention and continual effort. To look back while plowing was to risk deviating from the intended path, leading to inefficiency and potential failure in the task. Jesus was emphasizing commitment to the kingdom of God. Just as plowing requires dedication and focus, so does discipleship. The "looking back" He referred to is the way we get distracted by past attachments, regrets, or even comforts. It's a reminder that our walk with Christ requires our full attention, our unwavering commitment.

Jesus was highlighting the cost of following Him. Following Him is not a casual endeavor. It's a path and a purpose that demands our whole heart, our entire focus. We cannot move forward in our walk with Christ if we are constantly looking backward, holding on to our past. The call to follow Jesus is a call to a forward-focused, purposeful life, unhindered by the distractions and entanglements of what we've left behind.

This is a hard but freeing truth I've had to come to terms with. Especially because, historically, I haven't been the best steward. The truth is that I've certainly looked back and have even taken my hand off the plow. Heck, I've left the plow and walked in the opposite direction. But the important thing is,

I didn't dwell there. And if that's you right now, you don't have to dwell there either. I have to lay those attachments, regrets, and old comforts at His feet. I can't take them with me. I can't hold on to them and put my hand on the plow. I've got to let something go. Maybe you can relate to this too?

THE CALL TO FOLLOW JESUS IS A CALL TO A FORWARD-FOCUSED, PURPOSEFUL LIFE, UNHINDERED BY THE DISTRACTIONS AND ENTANGLEMENTS OF WHAT WE'VE LEFT BEHIND.

Looking back has its dangers. To consistently turn our eyes to the past is to risk losing our footing in the present. Yes, there might have to be sacrifices, moments of surrender, and things we've left behind to follow Jesus. But remember the call of our Savior. He doesn't just lead us away from something; He leads us toward Himself, toward a life more abundant than we can ever imagine. Toward harvests upon harvests.

The path there may not always be the easiest route, and it's often the one that is less traveled and less popular. It has its challenges, its valleys, and its mountaintops. Yet, it is the path that leads to everlasting life, to true fulfillment in Christ.

When we grasp our own plow—our God-given purpose in the now—we are saying a resounding yes to the Father's will. But, like anything, where our eyes are directed, where our heart's gaze is fixed, determines how faithfully we walk this path. If you find yourself burdened by the weight of yesterday, hear this gentle reminder: Jesus is here, in this very moment, as you are reading these black-and-white words on these pages, beckoning you to come to Him. Release the weight you've been carrying. Lay down those burdens at His feet. He is calling you to walk with Him, eyes forward, moving steadfastly onto the narrow path that leads to eternal life.

You won't walk this journey alone. With every step, He is with you. Take courage, hold tight to your plow, and let the promise of His presence and the hope of eternity guide you forward. Don't look back.

REFLECTION QUESTIONS

1. In what ways can we become so focused on future spiritual peaks that we miss the climb of daily experiences with God?

2. Reflecting on the parable of the ten bridesmaids, how can you prepare your spiritual oil to ensure you are ready for the unexpected delays in life's journey?

3. How have you experienced the tension between savoring the now and dealing with the distractions of the past or future?

4. What practical steps can you take to ensure that your daily walk with Christ is characterized by active engagement rather than passive waiting?

TEN

HEALING FROM THE SHADOWS OF REGRET

I (Britt) recognize a pattern of spiritual paralysis and regret that often circles back around in my life. It's as if time slips through my fingers, leaving me asking myself, *Where did all those days and months go?* I set goals, dream of great things, and then find myself standing still, not having taken the steps I intended. I'm struck by a sense of regret for the time I've let slip by, unutilized and stagnant.

Many might not know this about me, but I'm a musician. I've been a singer and guitarist since I was about ten years old. I've always had a love for singing and writing music. It's something I've had the privilege of sharing with my dad and my two brothers and has almost become a second language for us, a way to more deeply understand one another beyond words.

Music is a gift my Creator wove into my being for His glory.

Despite this deep connection to music, I've encountered periods where this gift felt underutilized, especially after I became a Christian.

The transition from secular to Christian music wasn't necessarily smooth for me. I started to associate the success of my musical ability with leading worship on grand church stages. This craving for recognition began to overshadow the pure joy of music that had once filled my heart. Everything shifted when I joined the worship team for college ministry. I never had the chance to lead. I was always put in the background. Doubt and feelings of rejection crept in. Was my talent lacking? These thoughts and, dare I say, insecurities tormented me. My longing for the spotlight revealed a prideful desire for recognition over true worship.

This came to a head one night, when another member of the team was chosen to lead at our worship event. There it was again, the stinging reminder of my deepest fears of inadequacy bubbling to the surface. I felt cast aside, unimportant, unseen— feelings that have felt all too familiar to me my entire life. I feared I was never enough, never measuring up, always missing the mark, unnoticed. It was a wake-up call when I found myself yelling at my dear brother Nick for not putting me in the leadership spot. He was the organizer of the set list and the musicians scheduled each week. I'll never forget the look on his face. He looked at me with compassion blended with confusion. I couldn't believe the words I'd heard exit my own mouth. I could almost see them floating in the air and wished I could take them back and erase them. I paused in my anger and heard this nudge clearly from the Holy Spirit: *Oh, boy. I'm in trouble here. I'm not doing this for the Almighty. I'm doing this for me.*

This wake-up call reflected some pretty ugly stuff in my heart. It was clear that my worship was not about devotion but a quest for applause so I would be seen by others as talented, anointed, and greatly used by God. Maybe the leader in charge of deciding who led worship saw this? Maybe he saw that I wasn't ready. Clearly, I wasn't. I realized I was in some deep inner turmoil. But God, in His loving-kindness, was working on my heart.

So what did I do next? Well, probably the wrong thing. I took ten steps back from music, realizing my heart wasn't aligned with God's will. Music, once an integral part of my identity, left me feeling lost without the validation I craved, and I didn't know how to keep at it without the validation, so it was easier for me not to do it at all. I didn't feel I deserved it anymore.

I'm walking through this with you because I allowed regret to close doors for me. But maybe it doesn't have to? Maybe pain and regret aren't the enemy here? Maybe they're an opportunity?

It's never too late to start anew, using our gifts to truly honor the Father. I've let regret hold me back long enough. Maybe you have too?

LET'S GIVE REGRET A NEW NAME

Regret is a tricky thing.

It's a word that often brings a sense of heaviness, isn't it? It feels like a heavy shadow trailing behind us, reminding us of what we could've or should've done differently. I (Britt) always think of the phrase "would've, could've, should've" in regard to regret.

Regret can come in all shapes and sizes. For me, most of it comes in the form of being inactive. Stagnant. Idle. Wasting time doing nothing. What could God have done through me had I been more available to Him? The regret goes on, and on, and on.

We're not meant to live in the shadow of regret. If we're going about our lives that way, what good will it do? How can we truly grow? Imagine trying to walk forward while constantly looking over your shoulder. You're not only going to stumble and run into things, but you're also going to miss what's right in front of you. Regret, when dwelled upon excessively, can paralyze us. It keeps us tethered to moments we cannot change, to words we cannot unsay, to choices we cannot undo.

But here's a thought: What if we could shift that feeling of regret into something different and more empowering? Something that doesn't chain us to our past mistakes, leaving us riddled with shame. What if, instead, we could see regret as a springboard for redemption and growth in Christ? What if, every time we thought about regret, we instead called it "grace-filled reflections"? Think about it! These grace-filled

REGRET, WHEN DWELLED UPON EXCESSIVELY, CAN PARALYZE US. IT KEEPS US TETHERED TO MOMENTS WE CANNOT CHANGE, TO WORDS WE CANNOT UNSAY, TO CHOICES WE CANNOT UNDO.

reflections are in no way stamps of failure. They're signposts pointing us toward wisdom and change.

Unlike the harshness and heaviness of regret, grace-filled reflections offer us a gentle nudge, a reminder that we're still learning, still growing, and still walking hand in hand with a forgiving and redeeming God. Regret and shame are used by the Enemy to force our faces away from God and to make us let go of His hand, but grace-filled reflections help us turn our faces toward Him with a willingness to be transformed. You see, pain isn't always the enemy we make it out to be. Pain can propel us into His arms.

Consider those moments you've labeled as regrets. Imagine them as grace-filled reflections instead. You'll notice that, as you rename them, they are no longer about your failures; they're about godly lessons learned. Each one is an opportunity to sit with God and ask Him, "What can I learn from this?" and, "Lord, how can You turn this into something good that brings You glory?"

Regret → Grace-Filled Reflections → Stepping Stones to a Deeper Understanding of His Unfailing Love for Me

So, together, let's flip the script. Our past doesn't have to be a burden. Instead, it can be a bridge. A bridge that leads us to a greater realization of our gracious Father, the hope He offers, and a deeper intimacy with Him.

Remember when Peter denied knowing Jesus (Mark 14:72)? Imagine the deep regret he must have felt afterward. Geez, if he had done that in today's culture, he'd be cancelled for life. This wasn't just some small mistake; it was a deeper significant moment for Peter. But the beautiful part of this? It wasn't the end of his story. Instead, it became a pivotal moment for him and one that led to great growth.

After Jesus rose from the dead, He had his heart-to-heart with Peter, asking him three times if he loved Him. This part always chokes me up. What a loving Savior we have! This wasn't just about getting Peter back on track. It was Jesus gently and lovingly helping Peter heal from his regret, giving him a chance to turn his biggest mistake into an opportunity for growth and to express his true love for the Lord (John 21).

And He does the same for us, friend. The Enemy doesn't want us to come to Jesus with our regret, shame, and pain. He wants us to stay hidden, lacking growth, looking over our shoulder. Fortunately for us, we know how his story ends.

HOW GOD SEES YOUR PAST

I (Britt) sometimes struggle with the concept of forgiveness and the idea that Christ can completely erase our past mistakes. My own past is a mix of good decisions and not-so-good ones, blessings mingled with missteps. Sometimes I lie awake at night staring at my ceiling, haunted by the "what if I hadn't" moments. Yet, when I reflect on my failings, I'm comforted by a powerful promise from Isaiah 43:25: "I, even I, am he who blots out your transgressions, for my own sake, and remembers your sins no more" (NIV). Though we may still struggle with beating ourselves up over our mistakes, we must come to a deep-down knowing that each layer of our past, though filled with failures, triumph, and even regret, has never made the Father turn away from us with crossed arms.

Let's look at the story of how Moses went from fugitive to deliverer. To give you a quick recap, Moses grew up in Pharaoh's palace but fled Egypt because he killed an Egyptian who was beating a Hebrew slave. He settled in Midian, married, became a shepherd, and essentially tried to start a new, quiet life far from the grandeur of Egypt. Moses' past was marked not only by his act of violence but also by his separation from both his Hebrew heritage and the Egyptian royalty who raised him. He was a man with a past he wanted to forget.

One day, he's out minding his own business, tending his sheep, probably thinking his palace days are way behind him, when he comes across a bush that's on fire but not consumed. God calls out to him from this fiery shrubbery and hits him with a life-altering mission: "Hey, Moses, you're going to free my people from Egypt." If I were Moses, I'd be looking around for the hidden cameras, because seriously? *Who, me? The guy wanted for murder? The one who's been hiding out in the desert?*

Here's the real kicker: God didn't dial the wrong number. He picked Moses on purpose. Moses even tried to back out, reminding God, "Um, You know I'm not exactly public speaker material, right?"

But God's like, "I've got this. I made your mouth, and I can surely make it say what it needs to."

This encounter blows my mind, because it shows us that God isn't looking for perfect resumes with spotless pasts. He's into using our mess-ups, our background, everything, and turning it into something beautiful.

I want to relieve you right now, friend. Your past isn't something you can change, but it's something that can change others if you're willing to let God use it. In light of this truth, let's not view our pasts as mere histories to be hidden away, but as testimonies of transformation. As we journey forward, it is crucial to understand that the God who worked through Moses is actively at work in us today. He doesn't just redeem our pasts; He repurposes them in a way that can bring hope and healing to others. Below is a list that doesn't simply offer bullet points for reflection but represents the profound and pivotal ways God can take the mosaic of our pasts and craft them into a masterpiece for His glory.

HE DOESN'T JUST REDEEM OUR PASTS; HE REPURPOSES THEM IN A WAY THAT CAN BRING HOPE AND HEALING TO OTHERS.

- **Your Past Doesn't Scare God Away.** Moses' background and his mistakes didn't disqualify him. In fact, they prepared him. All those years in Pharaoh's palace and then more years as a shepherd? Perfect training for what was to come. It's a reminder that where we've been can help us get to where we're going, especially when God is directing the way.

- **God's Not After Perfection; He's After Partnership.** Moses was far from the flawless-hero type, yet God chose him. It wasn't about Moses nailing it on his own; it was about him teaming up with God. Our biggest fails can be God's greatest wins within our story. We need only be willing.
- **Your History Has Purpose.** Every part of Moses' story, even the parts he probably wished he could erase, played a role in God's plan. It's comforting, right? Those parts of our stories we're not too proud of? God can use them too.
- **It's About the Heart, Not the History.** Moses' heart was what mattered. He was open, he was willing (eventually), and he let God lead. Our pasts might shape us, but it's our hearts that God is interested in.

Friend, know that you are free from shame and regret. You're set free not just to wander aimlessly, but to seize another chance to live out your God-given purpose right now. This freedom is a gift, an invitation to step forward into a life filled with purpose and a deeper connection to the One who will always love you unconditionally. Next time you're feeling a bit like a Moses, wondering how on earth God could use someone like you, remember the burning bush. Remember that God isn't in the business of collecting perfect people. He's looking for real, raw hearts open to saying yes to Him, even when it's hard. Even when we can't forget what we've done. The truth is that He's not tallying your rights and wrongs but inviting you on a journey with Him where every part of you, especially the broken parts, can play a role.

Take a deep breath in and a deep breath out, and imagine Him saying this to you:

I see you. I've always seen you. Every single part of you. Including those bits you're not too proud of. The ones you don't speak aloud. And you know what? None of it scares Me away.

I love you, all of you. There's nothing you can do that could make Me love you more, and there's nothing you could do that could make Me love you less. I love you, because I am love. I'm here with you, and I'm inviting you into something greater than you could even imagine.

Let go of the record of your failures. Place it at My feet where it belongs. I am the One who blots out your transgressions. I am the One who washes you clean. I am the One who set the stars in the sky and stretched out the seas below. In Me there are more than just second chances; there's an endless reservoir of grace.

REFLECTION QUESTIONS

1. When have you felt overlooked or underutilized in a role or ministry, and how did that experience refine your understanding of serving God versus seeking approval from others?
2. How has a past failure or mistake been repurposed in your life as a stepping stone for spiritual growth?
3. In what ways have you transformed regret into a positive force for change in your life?
4. What's one way God has used your past to prepare you for a specific task or mission He called you to?

CONCLUSION

It's an all-too-common tale, this idea that we're somehow not ready, not good enough, or not "something" enough to step into where God is calling us. I (Britt) myself have been trapped in the belief that, until I met certain criteria, I wasn't qualified to pursue my purpose. One area I find myself struggling to ignore is my weight; it is just not where I want it to be. When I fixate on that, it holds me back. It causes me to take myself out of the game. But I'm tired of living in this lie. That's what it is. It's a lie. It's a sneaky deception that I'm just one personal-improvement project away from being usable by God.

Honestly, as I write these words, I'm thinking, *Who am I to think that I'm unusable to the Creator of my very being?* I'm struck by the audacity of this lie. How dare I, or any of us, believe that we could ever be unusable by the One who meticulously crafted our existence?

If we were next to you right this moment, we'd place our hands on your shoulder and gently remind you of this: You cannot be disqualified by anything external when God has called you. You are free to start on the journey toward your purpose now, just as you are, because it's not about your ability but your availability to God's power working through you.

So, how about we drop the "when I . . . then . . ." mindset? Let's leave it at the feet of Christ. Because the truth is that we are ready as we are to step into purpose today.

You are ready as you are, at whatever weight.

You are ready as you are, even without permission.

You are ready as you are, even when you don't feel enough.

You are ready as you are, even if you've messed up.

You are ready as you are, before you graduate.

You are ready as you are, while you are single.

You are ready as you are, before you have kids.

You are ready as you are, without that job.

You are ready as you are, before you hit that milestone.

You are ready as you are.

STEP INTO YOUR PURPOSE NOW, NOT TOMORROW, AND NOT WHEN YOU HAVE WHATEVER IT IS YOU THINK YOU'RE MISSING, BUT TODAY, RIGHT WHERE YOU ARE.

As we come to the close of our journey together, we want to send you off with a heart full of hope and hands ready to work. The essence of our message is simple: Step into your purpose now, not tomorrow, and not when you have whatever it is you think you're missing, but today, right where you are.

As you get ready to take a step forward, here are a few take-aways for you.

- **Cherish the Tiny Moments.** It's in the quiet of our daily lives that God often speaks the loudest. Like when Jesus used a tiny meal to feed thousands (John 6:9–11), He uses our small acts in big ways.
- **Pursue Faithfulness over Flawlessness.** Remember, it's not about being perfect. It's about being present and saying, "Here I am! Send me" (Isaiah 6:8).
- **Say Yes to God's Nudges.** Don't let fear hold you back any longer. Just as Peter stepped out of the boat at Jesus' call (Matthew 14:29), step out even when the waters seem uncertain.
- **Shake Off the Stagnation.** Let's not be spiritual couch potatoes any longer. Faith without action is lifeless (James 2:26). Let's lace up our shoes and run that race set before us (Hebrews 12:1).
- **Live Intentionally Now.** This moment? It's your mission field. It's the only moment that matters, because it's the only moment you've got. Just as Esther was placed for "such a time as this" (Esther 4:14), so are you. Your purpose isn't on pause.
- **Heal and Step Forward.** Release the regrets. His mercies are new every morning (Lamentations 3:22–23).

Remember, your worth and your ability to fulfill your purpose are not dependent on external factors or self-improvement milestones. You are already equipped, already called, already loved, just as you are. Let us then approach each day with the confidence that God's strength is made perfect in our imperfections and His grace is sufficient for us, in whatever state we find ourselves.

So now, as we part ways in this book but not in spirit, may you carry forward the certainty that God is with you in your coming and going, in your waking and your sleeping, in your doing and your resting. You are standing on holy ground right now, wherever you are, because God is there with you.

May your heart be emboldened, your spirit enlivened, and your hands ready to serve in the unique ways only you can, reflecting the unchangeable love of our Creator. Go forth, not just with hope but with a commission. Live out the calling placed upon your life with joy and courage, knowing that in His eyes, you are already ready, already chosen, and infinitely loved.

We leave you with this benediction: May you feel the wind of the Spirit at your back, guiding you toward the purposes God has in store. May you walk in the assurance that you are never alone, for the One who calls you is faithful, and He will do it (1 Thessalonians 5:24 NIV). Take heart, dear friend, for in Christ, you are more than enough—you are triumphant because God is more than sufficient for you. The world outside your doorstep is ripe with opportunities for God to work through you. Will you give God your yes, just as you are? Step out now, not because all is perfect, but because His love has made it so.

MAPPING YOUR
DIVINE PURPOSE

Sometimes we're not totally sure what our purpose is to begin with, much less able to identify the everyday ways we can walk faithfully toward that purpose. And that's okay. We're here to help you get a clearer sense of that.

For the purposes of this exercise, take some time to reflect on what you find yourself doing often, what comes naturally to you, what brings you joy, and how you serve others. Then, grab a piece of paper and write out the statement below, filling in the blanks.

God has given me a gift of _____.

As a Bible-believing (son or daughter) of God, my role in the body is _____.

I currently feel called to serve by _____.

I am regularly giving of my _____ as part of this calling.

Here is an example.

God has given me a gift of <u>encouragement</u>. As a Bible-believing <u>daughter</u> of God, my role in the body is <u>counselor</u>. I currently feel called to serve by <u>listening to women express their struggles and offering support and biblical inspiration for their day-to-day lives</u>. I am regularly giving of my <u>time and emotional energy</u> as part of this calling.

This simple yet profound exercise serves as your compass, designed to align your daily actions with the greater purpose God has etched upon your life. As you continue to fill in these blanks and ponder your place within the grand narrative, remember that your purpose in God's kingdom is a tapestry woven from threads of your unique gifts, your heartfelt service, and the daily surrender of your resources to His divine will.

Take heart and take a step, no matter how small, toward that calling every day. Let this declaration be not just words on a page, but a living reality in your life. May it remind you that you are an essential part of the body, placed with care and intent by the Creator Himself. As you articulate your purpose, may you find clarity and conviction, and may your life reflect the light of His glory in everything you do.

FOUR BIBLICAL WAYS
TO ADDRESS OUR
NATURAL TRAUMA
RESPONSES

In a world rife with trials and uncertainties, our natural responses to trauma and threat—flight, fight, freeze, and fawn—can often leave us feeling powerless and exposed. Yet, we are not left defenseless. The Bible offers us profound insights and directives for such times, providing spiritual strategies to navigate and counteract these instinctual reactions. By delving into the Scriptures, we find not only solace but also empowering truths that equip us to confront our fears and stand firm in our faith.

Here are four ways to address each trauma or threat response through the power of Scripture and intimate relationship with the Lord.

FLIGHT—"RUN AWAY"

Scripture: "The name of the LORD is a strong tower; the righteous man runs into it and is safe." (Proverbs 18:10)

Reflect and Respond: When our natural response is to flee from danger or threats, it's comforting to know that we can always run to the Lord for protection. This proverb paints a beautiful image of God as our refuge, a safe place to escape when faced with overwhelming challenges.

FIGHT—"FACE THE THREAT HEAD ON"

Scripture: "Be strong in the LORD and in his mighty power. Put on the full armor of God, so that you can take your stand against the devil's schemes." (Ephesians 6:10–11 NIV)

Reflect and Respond: There will be times in our lives when the only option seems to be to face our challenges head-on. Paul reminded us that our strength comes not from ourselves but from God. When we clothe ourselves in God's armor, we're prepared to stand firm against any spiritual battles we may face. In this case, take your stand.

FREEZE—"BECOME PARALYZED IN THE FACE OF DANGER"

Scripture: "Be still, and know that I am God; I will be exalted among the nations, I will be exalted in the earth!" (Psalm 46:10 NIV)

Reflect and Respond: In moments of paralysis or indecision, this verse reminds us to take a step back and recognize God's sovereignty. Even in our stillness, there's an active trust and recognition of God's power. This psalm emphasizes that no matter the chaos or threats surrounding us, God remains unshaken, unchanging, and sovereign over all of it.

FAWN—"PEOPLE-PLEASING TO DEFUSE THREATS"

Scripture: "Am I now trying to win the approval of human beings, or of God? Or am I trying to please people? If I were still trying to please people, I would not be a servant of Christ." (Galatians 1:10 NIV)

Reflect and Respond: Paul's words to the Galatians act as a beautiful reminder that our ultimate aim should be to serve Christ and not simply to please others around us. While it may be our instinct to pacify others, our primary allegiance is to God, and His approval is what truly matters.

Through these four biblical responses to our natural reactions to trauma, we discover that we are not bound by our instincts but are liberated by the power of Christ. As we apply these scriptural principles to our lives, let us walk in the confidence that God's Word is the ultimate source of strength and guidance. In facing life's battles, may we always remember that our victory is secured not by might nor by power, but by the Spirit of the Lord (Zechariah 4:6). Let us move forward, therefore, not as victims of our circumstances, but as victorious children of God, fully equipped and eternally held in His grace.

THE REVERSING-REGRET FRAMEWORK

Regret doesn't have to hold us back. We've talked about renaming regret. Now let's reframe it. It no longer has to tether us or keep us frozen in yesterday. Let's expose every bit of regret so the Enemy can't use it as a tool against us. Try this journaling exercise.

Take a piece of paper and draw three columns. Label them "Regret," "Scripture," and "Small Step." Then fill out each column according to the directions below.

Regret: In this first column, write down a regret that's been heavy on your heart. Now that you have it written down, invite the Lord into it.

Scripture: In the second column, write down a passage from Scripture that speaks to that situation.

Reframe: In the third column, write down a small step you can take to reframe the way you see this regret.

I (Britt) will share my own personal example of the framework so you can see what we're talking about.

REGRET	SCRIPTURE	REFRAME
Wasting a decade being stagnant	"I will repay you for the years the locusts have eaten—the great locust and the young locust, the other locusts and the locust swarm—my great army that I sent among you." (Joel 2:25 NIV)	I can be assured of God's promise that He can and will restore what was lost and bring beauty and abundance out of my barren seasons.

Now that we've shifted our perspective, we need to enact a tangible shift in our daily walk. As we chart the course from what has happened to how we can move onward, we hold the pen that writes our future moments. Here, we transition from reflection to action, from what has been to what will be, with our eyes lifted heavenward and hearts attuned to the whispers of grace. How, then, can we embody this in our daily walk? How do we begin to live out the truth that our past can be a catalyst for God's transformative work in our lives and not a chain that holds us back?

HOW TO MOVE ONWARD WITH EYES UPWARD

- **Acknowledge and Accept.** Acknowledge what happened. Let it matter without letting it define you. Acceptance isn't about condoning what happened but recognizing it's part of your story and something God can use if you're willing.
- **Seek Forgiveness and Also Forgive Yourself.** If your actions hurt others or yourself, seek forgiveness. He is faithful to forgive us, friend. But don't forget to also extend that forgiveness to yourself. God's grace is sufficient for you (2 Corinthians 12:9), and His mercy is new every morning (Lamentations 3:22–23).
- **Spot the Lessons.** Every regret has a lesson hidden in it. Gracefully reflect on what happened, then pray and ask the Lord to show you what you could learn from it.

James 1:5 encourages us to seek wisdom from God, who gives generously to all without finding fault.

- **Step Forward in Faith.** Armed with the lessons and growth from your past, step forward in faith. Philippians 3:13–14 reminds us to forget what is behind and strain toward what is ahead, pressing on toward the goal to win the prize to which God has called us in Christ Jesus.

May you see your past through the lens of redemption, and may every small step you take be rooted in the truth of His Word and the steadfastness of His promises. The journey of reframing regret into purposeful action begins now—this moment is your starting line. Go forward with the confidence that in His hands, every experience, every regret, becomes a building block in the masterpiece He is creating with your life.

ACKNOWLEDGMENTS

BRITT

It's remarkable that this book has come to life, especially since so much of it started as personal reminders to myself—reminders to step out in faith, to stop hiding, to shake off the comfort of idleness, and to take bold steps even when fear and inadequacy whispered otherwise.

I'll never forget the moment God placed this message on my heart. Rocking my daughter in my arms, I asked, "Lord, what would You have me say to Your people if I had only one chance?" He showed me how many are immobilized—not from lack of desire, but from not recognizing their full potential in Him. Or worse, recognizing it but feeling paralyzed by inadequacy. He made clear the urgency of walking on purpose in this critical hour. We have never been closer to the Lord's return than we are today.

I must first acknowledge my Lord. For many years, I called Jesus my Savior, but I hadn't fully surrendered to His Lordship.

I stayed hidden out of fear because the immensity of where I felt Him calling me triggered deep inadequacy within myself. I've learned that it's actually less of me and my ability and solely Him and His surpassing power working through me. As the pressure came off, that's when I began to comprehend the significance of my life—and the significance of yours.

Ryan, my incredible husband and the better half of me, your unwavering love, encouragement, and selflessness have not only breathed life into this book but into every step of my walk. You've been my steady anchor when I felt adrift, my prayer warrior, and my loudest cheerleader. Your heart burns for people to encounter Jesus, and your relentless obedience to God's call amazes me every day. Walking beside you in this life and following where He leads you is an honor I cherish deeply. GGMY forever, babe.

Ariana, my sweet girl, you are my greatest gift and the heartbeat behind this book. Knowing that one day these pages will fall into your hands and reveal the powerful impact your life has for His Kingdom gave me the strength to press on. There are no words for how much I love you.

Cass, your fearless dedication to wherever God plants you is nothing short of inspiring. Your wisdom, honesty, and grace in these pages shine brilliantly. I have no doubt that countless hearts will be transformed by the power of Christ within them, revealed through your words and your breathtaking teaching of the Word.

Mom and Dad, words will never be enough to express how deeply grateful I am for both of you. Mom, your nurturing heart and endless sacrifices have shaped who I am today, always making me feel safe and cherished. Dad, your wisdom, guidance, and constant encouragement have given me the strength to pursue my dreams with confidence. Together, you've been my greatest safety net, and your unwavering belief in me has carried me. I am endlessly thankful for everything you've poured into my life and the love that has always surrounded me, no matter the distance or the circumstances.

My stepparents, Steve and Nia, thank you for embracing me with open arms, showing me love beyond blood, and demonstrating what true family looks like.

To my brothers, Ben and Nick, our bond is one my greatest blessings—woven with endless support, laughter, and the kind of humor that keeps me grounded and childlike, no matter how heavy life gets. Your love has been a constant source of strength, and your joy has carried me through. No matter where God takes us, we'll always be in it together.

Nanny and Papa H, your lives have been a beautiful testament to what it means to faithfully follow Jesus. Thank you for sharing that legacy with me and for witnessing to me at a young age.

Nanny and Papa R, you have always exemplified what it means to remain faithful to the very end—to endure through every season and to honor your vows with unwavering commitment.

Nicole, my sweet sister, you are a constant source of love and strength in my life. No matter what it is, you are always there. Your presence in every season is a blessing beyond words, I thank God every day for you and for your kind, caring heart.

Mallary, thank you for all our phone conversations when life gets hard. You've known me since I was thirteen years old and have seen just about every season of my life and stood by my side as my best friend regardless. Your selfless, kind heart and your fierce Mama love for your babies inspire me.

Angie, thank you for always celebrating with me and for offering such amazing wisdom, insight, and prayers. I love your heart for God.

Uncle Matt, no matter what, you're always there, and I'm deeply grateful to have you in my corner. You run to our rescue when things break and life hits. You've always been a pillar for me.

Lauren, you have an incredible gift for making me laugh in an instant. Your joy brightens my life, and I'm so grateful for the unwavering support you've always given me.

A very heartfelt thank you to Rachael Campbell, Amy Klutinoty, Jacob Zygmunt, the Todd Family, Lindsey Spear, Mariela Rosario, Savannah Labo, Paula Jauch, Bethny Ricks, Taylor Bruen, Olivia Loviska, Brittany Waite, Marcus and April Stanley, Allie Smith, and Ashley Robbins, you've each been a pillar in my life in ways I can never fully express. Your prayers, friendship, and unshakable support have carried me through, and for that, I'm eternally thankful.

To my precious nieces, Vanessa, Sophia, Kata, Rosie, Layla, Lucy, Maya, I pray that one day you'll read these words and know, without a doubt, just how valuable and cherished your lives are. You are each uniquely made, with a purpose that only you can fulfill. My prayer is that you will always walk in the confidence of knowing how deeply loved you are by God. Never forget that your lives hold immeasurable worth, and I am so blessed to be your aunt.

Jayden, my one and only nephew, you are an absolute joy in my life. The bond we share means the world to me. You never fail to make me laugh yet you have a depth to you that inspires me. I'm blessed to be your aunt and I can't wait to see all the amazing things God has in store for you.

To LifePoint church, your love and faithfulness to the call of God have been a constant source of strength and encouragement. Thank you for being the community that continually lifts us up in prayer and celebrates with us.

To the rest of all my family and friends, your love and support have meant the world to me. Thank you for standing with me every step of the way.

CASS

I must confess, there were numerous times I was tempted to give up and questioned whether this message should come from someone like me. The irony of writing a book like *Ready As You Are* while wrestling with defeat is not lost on me. The fact that you're holding this book in your hands is a testament to God's all-surpassing power at work in my weakness (2 Corinthians 12:9). If there's anything good that comes of this, all the glory goes to God.

First and foremost, to my husband, Dan—thank you for lending me your faith when mine was dwindling. Without you, nothing I do would be possible. You have this incredible ability to inspire me, even in moments of self-doubt. Your unwavering trust in God serves as a refuge and salve when life feels like it's kicking the crap out of me. Thank you for loving me so well. 1, 4, 3.

To my rowdy and wonderful children, Melody, Charlotte, and Everett—your handwritten notes, warm hugs, and the colorful pictures you drew during this process have been the encouragement that kept me going. Your support means the world to me, and I'm so grateful to be your mommy. You make every moment of this wild journey worthwhile.

To my Valor Village girlies, Bailey, Baleigh, Gabby, Grace, and Leah—thank you for inspiring so many of the words written in this book. I'm truly humbled to play a small role in your lives. You teach me far more than I could ever hope to teach you. Your courage and resilience light up my world, and I treasure each of you.

A special shoutout to my coauthor, Brittany Maher—thank you for your diligence and unwavering dedication to writing words that empower women to live on mission with God and participate in the Great Commission. Writing alongside you has been an incredible adventure, and I couldn't imagine this book without your brilliance.

Lastly, to my friends and family across the country—thank you for coming alongside me, bolstering me, and carrying me through with your prayers. I am especially grateful to my parents and my Denver Seminary WLC sisters for your encouragement during my private defeats and for celebrating each little victory as if it were your own.

A heartfelt thank you to Ainsley Britain, Alexandra Hoover, Ashley Abercrombie, Bethny Ricks, Chelsi LeBarre, Charaia Rush, Elizabeth Santelmann, Kelly Grantham, Kaylee Shaw, Sarah Hutcheson, Simi John, Stephanie Pompella Hutchison, Tabitha Panariso, and Ariana Rivera. I experience God's loving kindness tangibly through you, and I am beyond blessed to have you in my life.

TOGETHER

We want to extend our heartfelt thanks to our agent, Alexander Field, and our incredible team at The Bindery Agency—thank you for championing our words and helping us share the hope we have in Jesus with women everywhere. Your advocacy and belief in our message have been invaluable.

To our editors, Jessica Rogers and Janene MacIvor—thank you for shepherding our hearts and this book with such intentionality and expertise. We are deeply grateful for the guidance you provided throughout this process and for your unwavering support as we worked together. Your efforts have fortified our words and ensured we remain committed to our readers.

To our team at Nelson Books—thank you for investing in *Ready As You Are* and believing in its powerful message. Your hard work and dedication have made it possible for this book to reach countless women across the globe.

To our Her True Worth community—thank you for allowing

us to speak into your lives and be a part of your faith journey. It's a privilege we don't take lightly. We long for the day when we can meet you face-to-face, but for now we're grateful to be with you as you read the words on these pages. You inspired the words in this book.

NOTES

Chapter 3: The Little Things Do Matter

1. David Gate (@davidgatepoet), "Priesthood," Instagram photo, May 2, 2024, https://www.instagram.com/p/C6d-wTeu0Am/?img_index=1.

2. "Your Gifts: The Easy-to-Use, Self-Guided Spiritual Survey," Team Ministry: Gifted to Serve, https://gifts.churchgrowth.org/.

Chapter 4: Faithfulness over Flawlessness

1. *Merriam-Webster.com Dictionary*, s.v. "disqualify," accessed June 4, 2024, https://www.merriam-webster.com/dictionary/disqualify.

Chapter 5: Can I Really Do This?

1. Mary J. Evans, *Woman in the Bible: An Overview of All the Crucial Passages on Women's Roles* (InterVarsity Press, 1983), 45.

2. Craig L. Blomberg and Jennifer Foutz Markley, *Handbook of New Testament Exegesis* (Baker Academic, 2010), 53, https://web.archive.org/web/20050213180606/http://www.cbmw.org/sermon.php?id=22; https://www.merriam-webster.com/dictionary/egalitarianism. Linda Belleville, "Women in

Ministry: An Egalitarian Perspective," in *Two Views on Women in Ministry*, ed. James R. Beck (Zondervan, 2005).

3. Craig L. Blomberg and Jennifer Foutz Markley, *Handbook of New Testament Exegesis* (Baker Publishing Group, 2010), 53.

4. *Merriam-Webster.com Dictionary*, s.v. "egalitarianism," accessed June 4, 2024, https://www.merriam-webster.com/dictionary/egalitarianism.

5. Michael F. Bird, *Romans: The Story of God Bible Commentary* (HarperCollins Christian Publishing, 2016), http://ebookcentral.proquest.com/lib/dtl/detail.action?docID=5397790.

6. Toni Craven et al., eds., *Women in Scripture: A Dictionary of Named and Unnamed Women in the Hebrew Bible, the Apocryphal/Deuterocanonical Books and the New Testament* (Houghton Mifflin, 2000), xii.

7. Tom Wright, "Women Bishops: It's About the Bible, Not Fake Ideas of Progress," *Virtue Online: The Voice for Global Orthodox Anglicanism*, November 23, 2012, https://virtueonline.org/women-bishops-its-about-bible-not-progress-tom-wright-updated-retort.

8. Brittany E. Wilson, "Masculinity in the Greco-Roman World," in *Unmanly Men: Refigurations of Masculinity in Luke-Acts* (Oxford Academic, 2015), https://doi.org/10.1093/acprof:oso/9780199325009.003.0003.

Chapter 7: The Shape of Resilience

1. C. S. Lewis, *The Problem of Pain* (HarperOne, 2015).

2. Jamie Ivey, host, *The Happy Hour with Jamie Ivey*, episode 667, "Finding Hope in the Midst of Suffering with Jamie Ivey and Toni Collier," Ivey Media, May 3, 2024, https://podcasts.apple.com/us/podcast/hh-667-finding-hope-in-the-midst-of-suffering-with/id880741976?i=1000654425009.

3. John Mark Comer, "Dark Night of the Soul," *Practicing the*

Way, https://practicingthewayarchives.org/naming-your-stage -of-apprenticeship/step-sheet.

Chapter 8: Breaking Up with Idleness

1. James Clear, *Atomic Habits: An Easy and Proven Way to Build Good Habits and Break Bad Ones* (Avery, 2018), 17–18, Kindle.

Chapter 9: What Purpose Is There in This Very Moment?

1. Hope Reagan Harris, *Purpose Doesn't Pause: Finding Freedom from What's Holding You Back* (Esther Press, 2023).
2. Mark Batterson, *Win the Day: 7 Daily Habits to Help You Stress Less and Accomplish More* (Multnomah, 2023), xii.

ABOUT THE AUTHORS

Brittany Maher is a bestselling author and the founder and president of Her True Worth, a large and growing online ministry designed to liberate an entire generation of faith-filled women with the freedom found in discovering their true worth in Christ. She and her husband, Ryan, invest most of their time in equipping and empowering God's people for evangelism across the globe. Brittany is planted in Michigan with Ryan and their daughter.

Cassandra Speer is a bestselling author, sought-out Bible teacher, and vice president of Her True Worth. Her heart is driven by the desire to write words of hope and solidarity for the weary, wounded, and wandering woman looking for God. Cassandra and her husband are planted in Oklahoma City where they live with their three children.

Live *from* Your Worth, Not *for* It

THERE'S *beauty* IN YOUR BROKENNESS

90 DEVOTIONS
TO SURRENDER STRIVING, LIVE UNBURDENED,
AND FIND YOUR WORTH IN CHRIST

**Brittany Maher &
Cassandra Speer**
Leaders of the Her True Worth Community

This beautiful full-color 90-day devotional from founders Brittany Maher and Cassandra Speer of the popular online community Her True Worth weaves together original art, Scripture, reflections, and thought-provoking questions to help you embrace your complete identity and incredible value in Christ—even on the most overwhelming days.

ISBN: 9781400231195

Discover the woman you were meant to be when you find *your* worth in Jesus Christ.

her *true* worth

Breaking Free from a Culture of Selfies, Side Hustles, and People Pleasing to Embrace Your True Identity in Christ

Brittany Maher & Cassandra Speer
Leaders of the Her True Worth Community

Her True Worth is available wherever you buy books!
Learn more by joining the @hertrueworth community on Instagram!